3D Leadership
Designing Healthy Organizations

3D Leadership: Designing Healthy Organizations

Copyright © 2026 by Scott Williams

Published by 3D Leadership Consulting & Coaching

ISBN: 979-8-9954043-0-9 (paperback)

Printed in the United States of America

The experiences described in this book are drawn from the author's career in higher education leadership spanning more than three decades. Where specific situations are recounted, identifying details — including institutional characteristics, timing, and the particulars of events — have been altered or composited to protect the privacy of individuals. The leadership dynamics described are real. The individuals and institutions are not intended to be identifiable.

For permission requests, speaking engagements, or organizational use of this material, please contact:

scott@3DLeadershipCoaching.com

For the teams who showed me what healthy organizations look like from the inside.

Contents

A Note on Using This Book

3D Leadership is designed to be read and applied.

Each chapter closes with a set of reflection questions intended to help you connect the framework to your own organizational context. They are not abstract exercises. They are invitations to look honestly at the environment you are building and leading. Take them seriously. The most useful insights often surface in the honest answering of a simple question.

The book moves from foundation to framework to practice. Part I establishes why organizational health matters and what makes it possible. Part II explores each dimension of the 3D Leadership Architecture in depth. Part III examines how the architecture breaks down, how to read the signals of health, and how to build with intention.

You may read it cover to cover or move directly to the chapters most relevant to where your organization is right now. Either approach works. The framework will be clearest if you understand the foundation first, but each chapter is designed to stand on its own.

For the 3D Leadership Diagnostic, a structured assessment of your organization's current health, see Appendix B. It takes less than ten minutes to complete and will give you a clear picture of where your architecture is strong, where it is under strain, and where intentional attention will produce the greatest return.

For a structural view of how the dimensions interact and what the architecture produces when elements are present or absent in combination, see Appendix C: The Interdependent Equations.

Faculty adopting this book for course use will find a set of discussion questions for each chapter in Appendix D, designed for seminar and small group conversation across courses in leadership, organizational behavior, human resource management, and related fields.

Use the Diagnostic before you read, after you read, or both. The results will mean more once you understand the architecture behind them.

Introduction

Why Organizational Health Matters

The first two weeks of a new leadership role are pure observation. Every conversation is a data point. You are trying to learn the landscape quickly — the people, the politics, the unspoken rules — while projecting enough confidence that nobody notices how much you don't yet know. I arrived at the Career Center of a public research university carrying genuine excitement about what we could build together. The department had real potential: a large staff, a function that could command serious campus presence, and a mission that touched nearly every student who walked through the institution's doors. I could see what it could become.

I spent much of those first two weeks in meetings with deans and senior university leaders — introducing myself, beginning to build relationships, trying to understand how the Career Center was perceived across campus. The feedback I received was remarkably consistent. In meeting after meeting, from leaders across the institution, the same question surfaced in different forms. Some asked it directly. Others hinted at it politely. A few seemed genuinely puzzled that a department of our size existed at all.

"What does your department do again?"

The Career Center was known for one thing: the career fair. A high-profile, well-attended event that happened twice a year. Beyond that, as far as most of campus was concerned, the department quietly disappeared into the background. The reality was that we did far more than that. Career coaching. Employer relations. Graduate school preparation. Programming that ran year-round and touched thousands of students annually. None of it had registered. To the institution, we were essentially invisible.

I left those meetings each day carrying a complicated feeling: the excitement of seeing clearly what needed to change, sitting alongside the weight of understanding just how much work that would require.

Then I walked back into the office.

If the external meetings had revealed how invisible the department was to the rest of campus, what I found inside showed me why. The energy, or more precisely, the absence of it, was immediate and unmistakable. Staff members moved through the day going through the motions of work. There was motion without momentum, activity without engagement. Conversations were minimal. The atmosphere had a particular kind of quiet that felt less like focus and more like collective withdrawal.

I sat in on my first staff meeting with twenty-two people around the table or lining the walls of the room. I listened carefully. I watched. I waited for the natural rhythm of a team that cared about its work: the questions, the pushback, the small moments of enthusiasm that tend to emerge when people feel genuinely connected to what they're doing. Instead, questions were met with nods. Agenda items passed without comment. The meeting ended and people filed out without the easy exchanges that happen naturally in engaged teams.

The silence told me everything.

There were other signals. A team member seated with his back to the door, attention visibly elsewhere. He was present in the room but clearly attending to obligations that had nothing to do with the work at hand. Staff who came and went without clear purpose, moving through the day as if time were something to survive rather than use.

And then there was the moment that crystallized it.

One afternoon I left the building for a meeting with a dean that ran nearly ninety minutes. As I walked out, I passed a small group of staff members gathered near the bus stop at the entrance, taking a break. When I returned an hour and a half later, they were still there.

I didn't say anything. There was nothing useful to say in that moment.

These were not bad people. They were disengaged ones.

Disengagement of that depth doesn't happen overnight. It accumulates slowly, through years of unclear direction, inconsistent accountability, and an environment that had gradually communicated to people that their initiative wasn't needed and their contributions didn't particularly matter. A consulting review conducted before my arrival had documented the dysfunction in formal terms. The external reviewers had not been kind, and the findings confirmed what I could feel in the atmosphere every single day.

Though I was still developing my leadership vocabulary at the time, I understood clearly that what surrounded me wasn't a talent problem or a motivation problem. The people in that office were capable. Several of them would go on to demonstrate that convincingly once the environment around them changed.

What I was facing was a design problem.

The environment itself had produced these behaviors, and the environment would have to change before the behaviors could follow.

That understanding, developed through the leadership experiences that followed and refined through observation across many different organizations, is the foundation of this book. Because what I walked into that first week was not unusual. It was simply visible. Most organizational dysfunction is quieter, hiding beneath acceptable performance numbers and professional exteriors, living in the cautious meeting, the unasked question, the idea someone decided wasn't worth sharing. It accumulates in small withdrawals of energy and initiative until an organization is running on a fraction of its actual capacity.

The data reflects this pattern at a striking scale.

> Only 21% of employees worldwide report being engaged at work, meaning nearly four out of five employees are either disengaged or actively disengaged.
> — Gallup, State of the Global Workplace Report

> Fewer than half of employees say they trust their organization's leadership to do what is right.
> — Edelman Trust Barometer

If nearly 80% of employees are disengaged, the problem is not motivation. These numbers are not describing outliers or struggling organizations. They are describing the norm: most employees, in most organizations, moving through their workdays the way those staff members moved through theirs. Present, technically functional, and fundamentally disconnected from the work and from one another.

The challenge facing many organizations today is not effort.

It is organizational health.

Many organizations appear successful from the outside. They hit targets, grow, and produce the kind of performance metrics that look strong on paper and in annual reports. Inside the organization, however, the experience can feel entirely different. Energy fades. Conversations grow cautious. Initiative declines quietly, without fanfare, until one day leaders look up and realize the momentum they once had has been replaced by something harder to name but impossible to ignore.

Over the course of my career, I began noticing this pattern repeatedly, across sectors, across sizes, across organizations with vastly different missions and resources. Some were thriving. Some were surviving. Some were clearly struggling. Yet the underlying issue was rarely talent. Most organizations are filled with capable, hardworking people who care genuinely about the work they do. The difference was something less visible.

Healthy organizations operate differently. Trust allows people to contribute openly rather than cautiously. Direction provides clarity about what matters most and why. Culture encourages genuine collaboration rather than cautious self-protection. Leadership capacity extends beyond a small group of individuals at the top and lives throughout the system. When these elements align, organizations become remarkably effective. Energy increases, initiative expands, problems get solved rather than avoided, and momentum builds in ways that feel almost self-sustaining. When these elements weaken, even talented organizations begin to struggle. Work becomes harder than it should be. Progress slows. Engagement fades.

It was organizational health.

This book explores how leaders can intentionally build it.

The framework at its center is called the 3D Leadership Architecture, and it rests on a simple but powerful idea: healthy organizations emerge when three structural dimensions align on a foundation of trust. Directional Leadership provides clarity. Developmental Culture shapes how people work together. Distributed Capability expands leadership capacity throughout the organization. When these dimensions operate together, organizations become stronger, more adaptive, and more resilient under pressure. When they drift apart, strain begins to appear in ways that are predictable and preventable.

The chapters that follow explore each of these elements in depth — what they look like when they are functioning well, what happens when they begin to weaken, and how leaders can strengthen them intentionally within their own organizations. You will find examples from real workplaces, practical signals leaders can learn to observe, and clear ways to begin strengthening organizational health immediately.

Because what I learned standing in that office, watching twenty-two people perform the motions of work without the energy of genuine engagement, is something leaders encounter everywhere: in corporations and nonprofits, in universities and startups, in organizations with abundant resources, and in organizations running lean.

The problem is rarely the people.

It is the architecture surrounding them.

And architecture can be redesigned.

Healthy organizations are not accidental. They are built. Intentionally. Deliberately. Through leadership behavior practiced consistently over time. Every leader, regardless of title or position, has the ability to shape the environment in which people work.

PART I
The Problem

Chapter 1 — Performance Is Not Health

Strong results can mask fragile systems.

The leadership opportunity looked exceptional.

A prestigious research university. A well-resourced department with a strong national reputation. A senior leader who, by every visible measure, was exactly the kind of person ambitious leaders seek out. He was intellectually formidable, strategically sharp, and clearly respected at the highest levels of the institution. He had the president's confidence. He navigated complex academic politics with what appeared to be effortless skill. In the interview process, he spoke compellingly about student success, institutional impact, and the kind of bold vision that makes leaders lean forward in their chairs.

I accepted the role with genuine enthusiasm.

For a time, the results were undeniable. The department expanded. New initiatives launched. Employer engagement grew. The kind of metrics that matter in annual reports moved in the right direction. From the outside, and for a while, from the inside, it was momentum. The question was what it was costing.

But something felt wrong almost from the beginning. And it took me several months to understand exactly what it was.

The Words in the Room

Leadership team meetings at this institution had a particular atmosphere. My supervisor ran them with obvious command: prepared, articulate, and always several steps ahead of the conversation. That part was fine. What was unusual was the vocabulary.

He used words that stopped you mid-sentence. Not technical terms specific to higher education, those you expected. Uncommon words deployed with precision in ordinary conversation, words that sent your brain scrambling to reconstruct the meaning of what had just been said while the meeting continued moving forward around you.

I wasn't alone in the feeling. Others in the room noticed it too: the same quiet scramble to reconstruct meaning while the meeting moved on around them, the same effort to appear composed while privately playing catch-up. It was, I would come to understand, one of the more reliable signals of how the culture actually functioned: a room full of capable people, each quietly managing the same experience, none of them saying so.

A colleague said it plainly one afternoon. The language wasn't about communication. It was about control: a way of ensuring that everyone in the room remained just slightly off-balance, just dependent enough on the prevailing interpretation to stay quiet.

I remember the feeling when I heard that. It wasn't anger exactly. It was something closer to disbelief: that someone would go to those lengths, would study and practice an expanded vocabulary not to communicate more clearly, but to create distance. To make the people around him feel perpetually behind, perpetually catching up, perpetually dependent on his interpretation of what was being discussed.

Whether it was conscious strategy or simply the habit of a particular kind of intelligence, the effect was the same: his way always prevailed, because questioning it required first admitting you hadn't fully understood it.

The 4 AM Deadline

The phone rang on a weekday evening.

It was my supervisor. He had an early morning meeting with senior leadership. It was an opportunity to secure significant funding that had become available. He needed a full proposal.

He needed it by early morning.

There was no apology in his voice. No acknowledgment of what he was asking. It was stated as simply as if he were requesting a document be reformatted or a meeting rescheduled. "I need this by early morning. That should be fine."

I stayed up through the night and produced the proposal.

The concept was presented that morning. It was approved. The funding came through, and the program was developed. By any measurable standard, it was a success.

Fear, I learned that night, can produce results - but it comes at a cost.

That is precisely what makes fear-based leadership so difficult to recognize and so easy to rationalize. The proposal got written. The program got funded. The metrics looked fine. Nobody looking at the outcomes from the outside would have seen anything amiss. What they couldn't see was the cost: the late hours, the unspoken resentment, the growing understanding among the leadership team that their time and their judgment were not particularly relevant to the person setting the agenda. That cost doesn't appear in any report. But it accumulates. And over time, it shapes what people are willing to offer.

Performance and health are not the same thing.

The Moment I Pushed Back

There was a meeting in which my supervisor made a suggestion to the full leadership team. The idea was that students would benefit from working through the full institutional documentation available to them, a comprehensive approach to orientation that, in theory, made sense.

Around the table, heads nodded. Agreement settled into the room the way it always did. Quietly, without friction, without the kind of genuine discussion that might actually test whether the idea was sound.

I didn't nod.

I waited a moment, and then I offered a different perspective. Institutional documentation of that kind, I suggested, functions more like a car manual than assigned reading. When you purchase a new vehicle, you don't read the manual cover to cover before you turn the key. You refer to it when something specific comes up, when a warning light appears, when you need to understand a particular feature, when a question arises that requires a precise answer. The manual is a reference tool, not a curriculum.

The room was quiet in a different way than usual.

My supervisor considered it. And then — to his credit, and this matters — he took the feedback seriously. He engaged with the analogy. He didn't dismiss it or redirect the conversation back to his original position. Whatever his leadership style cost the team in other ways, he was capable of hearing a well-reasoned challenge when it was delivered respectfully.

I've thought about that moment many times since. I was the only one who spoke up. The others around that table were experienced, capable professionals. They had simply learned, through accumulated signals over time, that the effort of disagreement was rarely worth the cost.

That is what fear-based culture produces. Not incompetence. Not indifference. A learned calculation, operating just beneath the surface of every meeting, every conversation, every decision: Is this worth saying out loud?

When the answer is consistently no, the organization has already lost something it may not even know is missing.

What the Results Couldn't Show

The organization I was part of was not failing. By conventional measures, it was succeeding. It had resources, reputation, strategic positioning, and a senior leader who was genuinely talented in many of the ways that matter in complex institutional environments.

What it lacked was health.

Leadership meetings were tense beneath their professional surface. Expectations arrived without context or warning. Pressure moved downward and rarely invited the kind of candid exchange that produces better decisions. People performed well. They just didn't perform freely.

Over time, I understood that the environment wasn't going to change. Not because my supervisor was incapable of growth — that exchange suggested otherwise — but because the culture had calcified around his leadership style in ways that would take far longer to shift than I was willing to wait. Several opportunities had emerged that pointed toward something different, something with more room to build the kind of organization I believed was possible.

I left.

The organization I departed was not incompetent. It was intelligent, ambitious, well-resourced, and strategically positioned. It had talent, momentum, and institutional support. What it lacked was a healthy internal culture, the architecture that determines whether performance can be sustained or whether it will eventually consume the people producing it.

Over time, I came to understand a truth that experience has only reinforced:

Performance is not the same as health.

An organization can perform while quietly thinning its internal trust. It can grow while concentrating authority in fewer and fewer hands. It can win awards, hit targets, and produce programs that last for decades while exhausting the people responsible for all of it.

Three Kinds of Organizations

This pattern is not limited to high-performing organizations with hidden fragility. It appears across the full spectrum.

Some organizations are thriving: strong metrics, visible momentum, external validation yet quietly eroding the trust that makes sustained performance possible. The results look good. The internal experience feels increasingly strained. The gap between what the organization appears to be and what it actually feels like to work within it widens a little more each passing week.

Others are surviving because their market position or institutional standing protects them from the consequences of dysfunction. Demand remains strong. Competition is limited. Good enough continues to suffice until circumstances shift and the structural weakness that was always present suddenly has nowhere to hide.

Still others are struggling outright: low energy, stalled progress, fragmented communication, a leadership team that has stopped believing the work is going anywhere meaningful. The dysfunction is visible. What is less visible is that the cause is almost never the people.

Thriving. Surviving. Struggling.

In each case, the challenge is rarely a lack of talent or effort. Most organizations are filled with capable, hardworking people who care about the work they do. The issue runs deeper than individual performance.

It is the patterns of leadership behavior, cultural norms, and structural design that shape how the organization actually operates beneath its visible surface. How leadership behaves under pressure. How disagreement is expressed or suppressed. How capability is developed and distributed, or hoarded and centralized. How trust is reinforced over time — or quietly, incrementally, eroded.

I have led and observed under-resourced organizations that operated with remarkable cohesion, clarity, and collective purpose. I have also watched well-funded institutions fracture under the weight of their own internal strain. The difference was never ambition or talent.

It was organizational health.

The Question That Actually Matters

Organizational health determines whether performance compounds over time or eventually collapses under its own pressure.

The question, then, is not simply whether an organization is producing results. Results are visible, measurable, and easy to celebrate. They are also, as I came to understand, entirely possible in the presence of conditions that are quietly unsustainable.

The real question is whether the organization is healthy enough to sustain its results without consuming the people responsible for producing them.

Healthy organizations are not accidental.

They are designed.

Understanding organizational health, and learning how to build it intentionally, is one of the most important responsibilities of leadership. It is the work this book is about. And it begins, as most important things do, with understanding what we are actually looking at when we look beneath the surface of a functioning organization.

That is where we turn next.

PART II

The Three Dimensions

Chapter 2 — Understanding Organizational Health

Healthy organizations are rarely defined by their results alone. They are defined by the strength of the systems that sustain those results.

"Companies in the top quartile of organizational health are roughly three times more likely to outperform their industry peers."

— McKinsey Organizational Health Index Research

The Same Meeting, Two Different Organizations

Picture a Monday morning leadership meeting.

Eight people around a conference table. Coffee going cold. An agenda with four items, the first of which is a problem nobody has fully solved yet: a program that missed its targets last quarter, a gap between what the organization promised and what it delivered.

This meeting happens in two organizations simultaneously. Same agenda. Same number of people. Same problem on page one.

Watch what happens.

Organization A

The leader opens the meeting by acknowledging the missed targets directly. No spin, no softening. Just the number, what it means, and an honest question: "What are we seeing that I might not be seeing from where I sit?"

Someone speaks immediately. Not carefully. Openly. She's noticed a pattern in the data that points toward a structural issue rather than a performance one. The leader listens without interrupting.

Someone else builds on it. He's been watching the same pattern from a different angle and has a partial solution that might address one piece of the problem. He's not sure it's right. He says so.

A third person pushes back, respectfully, directly. She thinks the structural diagnosis is only half the story. There's a cultural piece too, and she names it even though it's uncomfortable, even though it touches on decisions made six months ago that people in the room were part of.

The room doesn't tighten. It leans in.

By the time the first agenda item closes, the original problem has been reframed, a working hypothesis has emerged that nobody walked in with, and two people have volunteered to follow up on specific pieces before the next meeting.

Nobody assigned them. They simply saw what needed doing and said so.

The meeting ends ten minutes early. People linger in the hallway, still talking.

Organization B

The leader opens the same meeting with the same missed targets. The number sits on the table like something nobody wants to touch.

Silence.

After a moment, someone offers a careful explanation — not quite an excuse, but close. It focuses on external factors, things outside the team's control. The leader nods. Another person agrees. A third adds a supporting detail.

Nobody disagrees. Nobody builds. Nobody reframes.

Around the table, two laptops are open. One person is checking her phone under the edge of the table with the practiced invisibility of someone who has done it many times before. The agenda moves forward.

The conversation that follows is technically functional. Information is shared. Updates are given. Decisions that have already been made are announced as decisions that are being made. People respond with nods.

The meeting ends on time. People leave quickly, separately, without lingering.

Later that afternoon, in a conversation that will never appear on any agenda, two colleagues process what they actually think about the problem in the first item: the real diagnosis, the uncomfortable piece, the thing nobody said out loud in the room.

They keep it between themselves.

These are not two different organizations.

They could be the same organization — at different points in its history, under different leaders, before and after something shifted in the trust people carried into that room.

The agenda was identical. The people were capable in both cases. The problem was real in both cases.

What was different was the environment.

In Organization A, people believed that speaking honestly was safe: that their ideas would be engaged rather than dismissed, that their concerns would be heard rather than managed, that the goal of the meeting was actually to solve the problem rather than to perform the appearance of solving it.

In Organization B, that belief had eroded. Nobody made a dramatic decision to stop contributing. It happened gradually, through accumulated signals: a comment that was dismissed, an idea that was ignored, a moment of honesty that cost someone something. Over time, people learned to calculate before they spoke. And eventually, many of them stopped speaking altogether.

That difference — between a room where ideas compound and a room where people quietly withdraw — is not a personality difference or a talent difference.

It is a trust difference.

The scale of what unhealthy organizations cost puts the stakes in sharp relief. Gallup estimates that employee disengagement costs the global economy roughly \$8.8 trillion in lost productivity annually, approximately 9% of global GDP. That number reframes the conversation entirely. Organizational health is not a soft concept, a human resources initiative, or a leadership philosophy reserved for organizations that can afford to think beyond their bottom line. It is one of the most significant economic issues of our time. The organizations that take it seriously gain a structural advantage.

Diagnosing Health Beneath the Surface

When an individual feels unwell, our health systems rarely diagnose based on appearance alone. Physicians look deeper — searching for underlying causes, identifying root issues, and prescribing treatment aligned with the actual condition rather than the visible symptom.

A person may look composed, attend meetings, hit deadlines, even perform at a high level — while underlying systems are quietly under strain. A person's health is not determined by outward productivity. It is determined by the wellness and coordination of internal systems.

In medicine, symptoms are signals. Fatigue, inflammation, elevated stress — these are not the illness itself. They are indicators that something beneath the surface is misaligned. Effective treatment begins with accurate diagnosis. Doctors do not treat fatigue alone. They ask what is causing it. The visible symptom is only the starting point.

Organizations function in similar ways. An organization can meet targets, expand programs, increase revenue, or gain recognition while internal systems quietly absorb strain. Trust erodes incrementally. Communication narrows. Decision-making centralizes. Conflict becomes guarded rather than constructive. The organization may still perform. But performance is not the same as health.

Organizational health is not measured by output alone. It is measured by whether leadership behavior, culture, and capability align in ways that sustain performance under pressure — not just when conditions are favorable, but when they are not.

And at the foundation of that design is trust.

Foundational Trust

Trust is a word leaders use often. They define it rarely.

In my experience, most organizations assume trust exists until something exposes that it does not: a difficult decision, a public failure, a budget cut, a leadership transition. Under pressure, the true condition of trust becomes immediately visible.

When trust is strong, disagreement remains constructive. Accountability feels fair. Communication stays candid. Even hard decisions are understood, if not always liked. People build on each other's ideas because they trust that contributing is safe.

The impact of trust is measurable and significant. In high-trust organizations, employees report 74% less stress, 106% more energy at work, and 50% higher productivity, along with significantly higher engagement and lower burnout (Harvard Business Review, The Neuroscience of Trust).

When trust is thin, pressure magnifies insecurity. Motives are questioned. Conversations narrow. People begin protecting themselves rather than contributing freely. Laptops open. Phones disappear under tables. The real conversations happen in hallways afterward, between people who trust each other individually even when they no longer trust the room.

Trust, in this sense, is not simply a feeling. It is a shared confidence in how the system operates.

The neuroscience of social threat and reward helps explain why trust operates the way it does in organizations — and why its absence is so costly.

The TERA Framework

The TERA framework was developed by Michael Bungay Stanier and introduced in his book The Coaching Habit, with further development in The

Advice Trap, both of which I highly recommend. Stanier drew on David Rock's SCARF model — a neuroscience-based framework that explains how the brain evaluates social situations as safe or threatening — and adapted those insights into a practical four-factor model that gives leaders a clear language for understanding why people engage or disengage. I draw on it here because it maps with remarkable precision onto what foundational trust either enables or quietly destroys in organizations.

Research on social threat and reward responses shows that human beings are constantly, and largely unconsciously, scanning their environment for signals along four dimensions: Tribe, Expectation, Rank, and Autonomy. Together they determine whether people experience their environment as safe enough to engage fully or threatening enough to require self-protection.

Tribe

Tribe refers to our need for belonging, the sense that we are part of a group that includes us, values us, and has our back. When tribe is strong, people feel connected to their colleagues and to the mission. When tribe weakens, isolation grows. People begin to feel that they are operating alone, that the organization's success and their own success have quietly become separate things.

In the Monday morning meeting, the people in Organization A experienced strong tribe. They were genuinely working together toward a shared outcome. The people in Organization B experienced something different — physically together but psychologically separate, each managing their own position rather than contributing to a collective solution.

Expectation

Expectation refers to clarity: knowing what is expected, how decisions get made, and what behavior the environment rewards. When expectations are clear and consistent, people can focus their energy on the work itself. When expectations are unclear or shift without warning, anxiety rises and people spend increasing amounts of energy trying to read the environment rather than contributing to it.

Leaders who assume their teams understand expectations are often surprised by the gap between what they believe they have communicated and what their teams have actually internalized. Clarity is not the absence of complexity. It is the presence of consistent, honest communication about what matters most and why.

Rank

Rank refers to our sensitivity to status and respect: the sense that we are valued, that our contributions matter, that we are seen as capable and worthy of trust.

The leader described in Chapter 1 illustrated this dynamic with precision. His use of uncommon vocabulary was, at its core, a rank signal: a way of establishing that his position in the intellectual hierarchy of the room was not subject to challenge. The effect was that everyone else's rank felt perpetually diminished, and the quality of thinking in the room suffered accordingly.

This is not about ego. It is about the deeply human need to feel that our presence in the room is an asset rather than a liability. When rank feels secure, people contribute freely. When rank feels threatened, by dismissal, by public correction, by subtle signals that some voices matter more than others, people protect themselves. They stop sharing ideas that might be wrong. They stop asking questions that might reveal gaps. They perform competence rather than exercising it.

Autonomy

Autonomy refers to our need to have some degree of control over our own decisions and our own work: the sense that we are trusted to exercise judgment, that we are not simply executing someone else's decisions but genuinely contributing to outcomes that matter.

When autonomy is present, people take ownership. They bring initiative. They solve problems rather than waiting to be told how to solve them. When autonomy disappears, when every decision requires approval, when initiative is regularly second-guessed, and when people learn that their judgment is not trusted, disengagement follows with remarkable predictability.

The staff members in the department I described in the introduction had not always been disengaged. Disengagement is rarely a choice people make consciously. It is what happens when, over a long enough period of time, all four TERA signals point in the wrong direction. Tribe weakens. Expectations become unclear. Rank feels unacknowledged. Autonomy disappears. Eventually, the environment communicates something unmistakable: your full engagement is not needed here.

People respond to that signal rationally. They give what the environment asks for, which is considerably less than what they are capable of.

Foundational trust is what keeps all four TERA signals pointing in the right direction. It is the belief, earned through consistent leadership behavior over time, that the organization will operate with integrity, that contributions will be valued, that disagreement is safe, and that accountability is fair.

It is not agreement. It is not comfort. It is not the absence of tension.

It is the confidence that the system can be trusted — even when the stakes are high, even when the news is bad, even when the meeting starts with a number nobody wants to look at.

Without foundational trust, culture adapts. People adjust. Performance may continue for a time. But as strain accumulates, the gap between what the organization could be and what it actually is grows wider.

With foundational trust, pressure does not destabilize the organization.

It clarifies it.

The 3D Leadership Architecture

Trust is the foundation. But foundation alone does not make a building. It makes a starting point.

Healthy organizations require more than trust. They require clarity in direction, strength in culture, and capability developed throughout the organization — not concentrated at the top, not assumed to exist, but intentionally designed and consistently reinforced.

Organizational health, therefore, is not the result of good intentions or fortunate circumstances. It is the product of design.

This framework is called the 3D Leadership Architecture. It is built on trust and strengthened through three structural dimensions: each distinct, each essential, and each dependent on the others to function at full strength.

Directional Leadership

Directional Leadership establishes clarity. It defines purpose, sets expectations, aligns strategy, and models the behavior leaders hope to see throughout the organization. It answers the question every team member is quietly asking: Where are we going, and how will we operate along the way?

Developmental Culture

Developmental Culture shapes how people work together day to day. It reinforces trust, encourages constructive disagreement, strengthens communication, and creates an environment where individuals feel safe contributing fully. It answers the question: How do we function together — not in policy, but in practice?

Distributed Capability

Distributed Capability ensures that leadership strength extends beyond a small group of individuals at the top. It intentionally develops people across roles and levels through career growth, leadership development, and mentorship. It answers the question: How do we develop leadership at every level, not just at the top?

These dimensions are distinct but deeply interdependent.

Direction without culture becomes rigid: clear priorities enforced through compliance rather than commitment, producing results that are brittle under pressure.

Culture without direction becomes unfocused: warm relationships and genuine engagement pointed at too many things at once, generating energy without momentum.

Capability without either becomes fragmented: talented individuals developing skills in an environment that doesn't know where it's going or how it wants to operate, eventually taking those skills somewhere else.

When all three align on a foundation of trust, however, something different emerges. Direction clarifies priorities. Culture reinforces behavior. Capability sustains momentum. The architecture itself begins supporting performance rather than straining against it.

Remove any one dimension and the structure weakens. Neglect the foundation and even strong dimensions begin to fracture. But when all elements are present and aligned, organizations become remarkably resilient — able to absorb pressure, adapt to change, and sustain performance not because conditions are always favorable, but because the architecture is sound.

Healthy organizations are not defined by a single strength.

They are defined by alignment across the system.

The Three Dimensions Are Interdependent

It is worth noting from the outset that the three dimensions of the 3D Leadership Architecture do not operate in isolation. They grow together and reinforce each other.

Strong direction gives culture something to grow toward. A healthy culture creates the conditions in which capability can be developed and distributed. And as capability expands across the organization, direction becomes easier to execute because more people are equipped to carry it forward. Foundational trust, the base on which all three dimensions rest, either amplifies or undermines the entire system.

This interdependence is important to understand because it shapes how organizational health is built, and how it breaks down. When the architecture is functioning well, each dimension strengthens the others, and the organization develops resilience it did not have before. When one dimension weakens, the strain is felt across the system. We will explore what that looks like in practice in Chapter 6.

For now, the key insight is this: organizational health is not the sum of three independent efforts. It is the product of three dimensions working together.

For a structural view of how these dimensions interact and what the architecture produces when elements are present or absent in combination see Appendix C: The Interdependent Equations.

Leadership Reflection

Consider the organization you lead, or the one you are part of, through the lens of what you have just read.

Think about the last significant meeting you attended. What actually happened in the room.

Now consider the four TERA conditions in your organization.

There are no neutral answers to these questions. Every organization sits somewhere on each dimension, and the honest answers reveal far more about organizational health than any performance metric can.

The architecture of a healthy organization begins with understanding where you actually are — not where you intend to be, not where the last strategic plan said you would be, but where the people in your organization experience themselves to be every day.

That is the starting point for everything that follows.

Chapter 3 — Developmental Culture

The Catalyst Dimension

Culture is not what organizations say they value. It is how people behave when pressure appears.

> "Culture eats strategy for breakfast."
> — Often attributed to Peter Drucker

That phrase has traveled far. You have likely heard it in a leadership meeting, seen it on a slide deck, or encountered it in a book much like this one. It captures something true — that culture is powerful, that it shapes outcomes in ways strategy alone cannot.

But I would frame it differently.

Culture sets the breakfast table and invites Strategy to sit down.

If the table is unstable — built on thin trust, guarded communication, and the quiet understanding that honesty carries risk — even the best strategy will struggle to gain traction. People will nod at the plan and then return to the behaviors the environment has trained them to exhibit. If the table is steady — built on trust, shared purpose, and the genuine belief that contributions matter — strategy becomes far easier to execute. Not because the plan is better, but because the people carrying it forward are fully present.

Culture does not replace strategy. It determines whether strategy works.

I have held a belief throughout my leadership career that I want to state plainly here, because it is relevant to everything that follows: of the three dimensions in the 3D Leadership Architecture, culture is the catalyst.

It does not replace Directional Leadership or Distributed Capability. It creates the conditions in which both can function at their full potential. Direction can be communicated clearly, but without a strong culture, it will be received with skepticism rather than commitment. Capability can be developed intentionally, but without a strong culture, it will be underutilized or lost entirely as people take their talents somewhere they feel more valued.

Culture is what makes the other dimensions real rather than theoretical. In a strong culture, people feel safe enough to ask openly for direction rather than guessing at it. They feel trusted enough to voice their development needs rather than concealing their gaps. They feel connected enough to the mission that they invest in the organization's success as if it were their own.

When culture weakens, the other dimensions weaken with it — not because direction or capability disappears, but because the environment no longer supports the honest communication and genuine engagement those dimensions require. When culture is strong, direction lands with clarity and capability develops with confidence.

Culture is the soil in which everything else either grows or doesn't.

Culture Is Behavior

In leadership conversations, culture is often described in abstract terms: values statements, posters on office walls, phrases repeated during onboarding and forgotten by the second week.

But culture is not an aspiration.

Culture is behavior.

It is revealed not in what organizations say they value but in how people actually act when deadlines tighten, when priorities shift, when problems surface that nobody anticipated. It appears in the everyday patterns that most leaders never consciously designed: how people communicate when they disagree, how leaders respond when someone delivers bad news, how individuals treat one another when outcomes matter and pressure is high.

Culture becomes visible not in moments of comfort, but in moments of strain.

The researcher who has done perhaps the most important work on this question is Amy Edmondson of Harvard Business School. Her decades of research on psychological safety, the shared belief that a team is safe for interpersonal risk-taking, has demonstrated something both simple and profound: teams with high psychological safety demonstrate significantly higher learning and innovation behaviors than those without it. Not marginally higher. Significantly.

What Edmondson found, across industries and organizational types, is that people perform better when they believe it is safe to speak up, to ask questions, to admit mistakes, and to challenge assumptions — without fear of punishment or humiliation. Psychological safety is not about being comfortable or avoiding hard conversations. It is about creating the conditions in which honest, productive work can actually happen.

That is precisely what developmental culture builds.

Healthy cultures do not eliminate tension or protect people from difficulty. They make tension productive. They create the conditions in which difficulty leads to growth rather than withdrawal, and in which accountability feels fair rather than punitive.

Trust, as we explored in Chapter 2, is what allows people to contribute without constantly calculating risk. When trust is strong, people spend their energy on the work. When trust is thin, they spend it on self-protection. The difference between those two states is not subtle — it is the difference between an organization running at full capacity and one running at a fraction of it.

What a Developmental Culture Looks Like

For many years, I led the Career Center at a large public research university. I did not arrive to a healthy culture. As I described in the introduction, I walked into an environment of visible disengagement — staff members going through the motions, a department invisible to the institution it served, and a consulting report that confirmed in formal terms what the atmosphere communicated every day.

What emerged over the years that followed was something entirely different.

The department had grown into one of the most engaged teams I have encountered anywhere in my career — not because we had exceptional talent that fell from the sky, but because we built something intentionally over time. We built a culture where people felt trusted to do their work. Where innovation was not just tolerated but actively celebrated. Where the energy in the building on a Monday morning felt genuinely different from the organizations around us.

I want to be honest about something. I am proud of the measurable outcomes sustained over a decade, the national recognition, the programs that grew far beyond anyone's initial expectations. Those results matter, and they represent the work of an extraordinary team.

But the feeling of going to a vibrant workplace every day was even better than the numbers.

That is not a soft statement. It is the point. Performance metrics tell you what an organization produced. The feeling in the building tells you whether it is sustainable — whether the people producing those results were growing, contributing, and fully invested in what they were doing. We had individuals who grew into responsibilities that surprised everyone, including themselves. We had a room, on any given day, that felt alive with the energy of people who believed in what they were doing and trusted the people around them.

That didn't happen by accident. It happened by design.

Building Culture Intentionally

One of the principles I returned to throughout my time leading that department is deceptively simple: you cannot sell innovation, sit back, and let it happen organically. You have to take intentional steps to grow it. The same is true of culture itself.

Culture requires reinforcement. It requires structures, rituals, and consistent leadership behavior that sends the same signal, over and over, until that signal becomes part of how the organization understands itself.

One of the structures I am most proud of was our annual Innovation Summit.

Every member of the department, more than thirty people, gathered for a morning dedicated entirely to ideas. Each person had roughly three minutes to deliver an elevator pitch for something new: a program, a process improvement, a solution to an existing challenge, a best practice borrowed from another institution and adapted for our context. The format gave every voice equal footing. The newest staff member had the same platform as the most senior. Every idea received the same respectful attention.

The environment was designed to be supportive, not evaluative. The goal was not to filter ideas but to generate them — to communicate clearly and repeatedly that innovation was something the organization valued, and that every person in the room was considered capable of contributing to it.

Many of those ideas were implemented. Some became signature programs that grew to serve thousands of participants annually and earned national recognition. Several became models that peer institutions studied and replicated. They started as someone's three-minute idea in that room.

What the Innovation Summit did beyond generating programs was something harder to measure but equally important. It told people, consistently and annually in a visible and celebratory way, that their thinking mattered. That leadership wasn't the only source of good ideas. That the organization's future was something everyone had a hand in shaping.

That is what intentional culture looks like in practice.

Not a values statement.

A room full of people who believe their contributions are genuinely wanted.

Protecting the Team

One of the quieter responsibilities of leadership — rarely discussed in books, rarely listed in job descriptions — is the work of buffering your team from the disruption that flows down from above.

Every leader who operates within a larger institution knows what I am describing. Directives arrive from senior leadership: policy changes, restructuring decisions, new priorities that land without warning or context. In many organizations, those directives cascade directly to staff, who experience them as anxiety-producing uncertainty with no guidance on what they mean or how to respond.

I made a deliberate practice of getting ahead of those moments.

When a significant directive arrived, my first priority was to understand it well enough to explain it honestly before my team encountered it on their own. I would gather the leadership team, discuss the challenges openly, and make clear how our department was going to navigate it. Not spin. Not false reassurance. An honest account of what was happening, what we knew, what we didn't know, and what our response was going to be.

The effect of that practice was significant. Not because it eliminated uncertainty — it didn't — but because it communicated something essential to the people on the team: you are not alone in this, leadership is paying attention, and we will face it together.

That is what trust looks like under pressure. Not the absence of difficulty. The confidence that the organization will function with integrity when difficulty arrives.

When Culture Produces Results

Perhaps the most tangible evidence of what developmental culture produces is not a philosophy or a framework. It is what happens when you hand a room full of engaged, trusted people a real problem and ask them what they think.

For years, the department hosted career fairs that were recognized across the industry as high-quality, high-impact events delivered at significant scale. We were proud of them. But pride, in a developmental culture, is never a reason to stop improving.

After every major fair, we gathered the full team for a debrief. Not a review led by leadership. A genuine open conversation: what went well, what could be better, what did we notice that we hadn't anticipated. The belief underlying that practice was simple: small improvements, compounded over time, produce big results. And the people closest to the experience are often the ones who see the clearest path to making it better.

The staff bought into that belief completely. Over time, their ideas transformed what had already been a strong event into something genuinely exceptional. They redesigned the student check-in process to reduce bottlenecks. They enhanced the preparation area. They introduced tours on the hour for attendees experiencing the event for the first time. They added a professional photo booth because participants were already dressed for the occasion, and a quality headshot in that moment had real practical value. They created a practice pitch area where participants could rehearse their introductions before approaching employers.

None of these ideas came from a strategic planning retreat or a leadership directive. They came from staff members who felt trusted enough to observe, think, and speak up — and who believed that when they did, something would actually happen.

Something did.

The event became a benchmark. A major industry vendor requested permission to attend and observe — not to exhibit, but to study what we had built. Peer institutions benchmarked our practices and implemented them at their own organizations. Programs that began as staff suggestions in a post-event debrief became models for peer organizations elsewhere in the field.

That is what developmental culture produces when it is genuinely operating. Not just engagement scores or retention rates. Tangible, exportable excellence — built from the ground up by people who trusted that their ideas were worth sharing.

Culture at Scale

Some organizations have demonstrated the power of developmental culture not just in a single department but across thousands of locations and tens of thousands of employees.

Consider Costco. In one of the most competitive and margin-thin sectors in retail, Costco has built something that most of its competitors have not: a workforce that stays. Employee turnover at Costco runs dramatically below industry averages, and the company consistently ranks among the most productive retailers in the world on a per-employee basis. The explanation is not complicated. Costco made deliberate architectural decisions about wages, about development, and about promoting from within that sent a consistent signal to every employee about what the organization actually valued. That signal, repeated over decades, became culture. And that culture became a structural advantage that competitors could not easily replicate by copying any single policy.

Costco didn't accidentally build a great culture. They designed one.

Mayo Clinic offers a similarly instructive lesson in a very different context. For more than a century, Mayo has sustained a single guiding principle: the needs of the patient come first. Through leadership transitions, technological transformation, and growth into one of the largest and most complex healthcare organizations in the world, that principle has remained the consistent signal the culture sends to every person who joins it. It shapes how physicians collaborate across specialties, how decisions get made under pressure, and how the organization has maintained its reputation for excellence across generations of leadership.

That is not an accident of mission. It is the result of deliberate, sustained architectural decisions about what the organization actually values — decisions reinforced consistently enough that they became the culture itself.

The lesson in both cases is the same: culture is not what organizations say they value. It is the sum of the decisions leaders make, repeated consistently over time, that tell people what the organization actually values. When those decisions point toward trust, development, and genuine belonging, culture becomes the organization's most durable competitive advantage. When they don't, culture becomes the organization's most persistent liability.

Signals of a Healthy Culture

When developmental culture is genuinely strong, it becomes visible in the everyday texture of organizational life — not in reports or surveys, but in what you see and feel when you walk through the door.

People take initiative. Team members volunteer for assignments, step forward when a colleague is stretched thin, and bring ideas to problems that aren't technically their responsibility to solve.

Engagement becomes visible and audible. Staff contribute ideas in meetings. They ask genuine questions. They push back constructively when they see a better path.

Informal connection flows naturally. Conversation happens easily — sometimes about work, sometimes about the small details of each other's lives that remind people they are working alongside human beings rather than job titles.

Collaboration becomes the default rather than the exception. People seek each other out not because an org chart requires it but because they trust one another's thinking and want the benefit of it.

These signals may appear small taken individually. Collectively, they represent something significant: people feel safe enough to be fully present.

When Culture Begins to Weaken

Cultural decline rarely announces itself dramatically. It appears first in small behavioral shifts that are easy to dismiss individually but unmistakable in pattern. Doors close — literally. Where offices were once open and conversation flowed easily, people begin shutting themselves away. Meetings grow quieter. Participation fades.

Complaints begin to replace collaboration. Instead of solving problems together, frustration circulates in small private groups — the hallway conversations after the meeting, the messages between trusted colleagues about what they didn't say out loud in the room.

Energy declines. The enthusiasm that once characterized the work fades into something flatter and more guarded.

The leaders who catch these signals early enough to respond have a significant advantage over those who wait until the dysfunction is visible in performance data. By the time culture shows up in the numbers, it has usually been declining for a long time.

Culture Must Be Actively Reinforced

Healthy cultures do not sustain themselves automatically. They require consistent reinforcement through leadership behavior, structural practices, and the daily signals that accumulate over time into something people either trust or don't.

The Innovation Summit was one structure. Weekly staff meetings that included intentional recognition, a simple practice of acknowledging each other's contributions publicly, were another. A culture committee that planned events, professional development opportunities, and informal gatherings that strengthened relationships across the team was a third.

None of these were complicated. None required significant resources. What they required was consistency — the willingness to keep showing up with the same message, year after year, until the message became part of how the organization understood itself.

The message was simple: the people in this organization matter, the work matters, and we are going to treat both accordingly.

When individuals feel genuinely valued and connected to the work, and to one another, engagement rises naturally. And when engagement rises, initiative follows. Problems get solved earlier. Ideas emerge from unexpected places. People grow into responsibilities that once seemed beyond them.

Culture, built this way, becomes the organization's most powerful engine of performance. Not because it replaces accountability or strategic clarity, but because it creates the conditions in which both can actually work.

Leadership Reflection

Consider the culture within your organization — not the values on the wall, but the behaviors in the room.

If the honest answers to most of these questions are encouraging, your culture is likely functioning as a genuine asset. If they reveal gaps — if the meeting is quiet, if initiative is rare, if informal connection has faded — the culture may be weakening in ways that have not yet shown up in your performance data.

Culture rarely changes through policy alone. It changes through leadership behavior — through the consistent, daily signals that tell people what the organization actually values and whether they are truly part of it.

The work of building developmental culture is not complicated. But it requires something that no strategic plan can manufacture.

It requires showing up the same way, day after day, until people believe you mean it.

Chapter 4 — Directional Leadership

The Alignment Dimension

Clear direction aligns effort.

On September 12, 1962, President John F. Kennedy stood before a crowd of forty thousand people at Rice University in Houston, Texas, and said something that had never been said by any national leader before.

> "We choose to go to the moon in this decade and do the other things, not because they are easy, but because they are hard."

Seven words: "We choose to go to the moon."

At the time, the United States had logged a grand total of fifteen minutes of human spaceflight. The Soviet Union was ahead in virtually every measurable dimension of the space race. NASA was a young agency still learning how to safely launch a human being beyond the atmosphere, let alone return one from a quarter million miles away. The engineering challenges were staggering, many of them not yet fully understood. The timeline, one decade, was extraordinarily ambitious.

And yet something remarkable happened after that speech.

Thousands of scientists, engineers, and support staff — many of whom could have worked anywhere, for anyone — oriented their entire professional lives around a single, audacious goal. Not because they were ordered to. Not because compliance was enforced. But because the direction was clear enough, and the mission compelling enough, that people chose to commit.

That is the difference between compliance and commitment.

Compliance completes tasks. Commitment moves organizations forward.

The Apollo program succeeded not because every person working on it was told exactly what to do, but because every person working on it understood exactly what they were working toward. Direction of that clarity does not constrain people — it liberates them. It tells them where to focus their creativity, their energy, and their problem-solving. It answers the question that every engaged employee is unconsciously asking every day: does what I do here actually matter, and to what end?

When leadership cannot answer that question clearly, the cost is not neutrality. It is drift.

What Happens Without Direction

The absence of clear direction is rarely dramatic. Organizations do not typically collapse overnight because no one knows where they are headed. They drift. Slowly, quietly, and at significant cost.

Effort fragments. In the absence of a shared destination, individuals and teams optimize for what they can see and control: their own priorities, their own interpretations of what matters, their own definitions of success. Work gets done. Tasks are completed. Meetings are held. But the cumulative energy of the organization scatters rather than compounds.

That fragmentation carries a measurable cost. Studies estimate that employees lose the equivalent of $6,650 per year per person trying to decode communications from managers and co-workers (Harris Poll/Box of Crayons, Navigating a Fractured Workplace, 2024).

A useful thought experiment: imagine an organization of fifty talented, motivated people, each working genuinely hard, each contributing meaningfully to their own function. Now imagine those fifty people pulling in seventeen slightly different directions because no one has given them a clear and common destination. The raw capacity is substantial. The collective output is a fraction of what it could be.

Direction does not add talent to an organization. It aligns the talent that already exists.

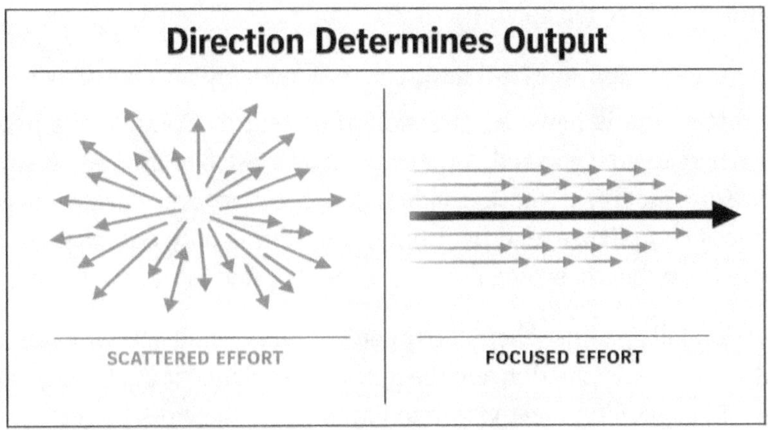

There is also a subtler cost to directional absence that shows up not in performance data but in engagement. People who care about their work, who are genuinely invested in doing something that matters, become quietly demoralized when they cannot connect what they do each day to where the organization is going. It is not that the work becomes harder. It is that it starts to feel less meaningful. And when work feels less meaningful, the most talented and motivated people — those with the most options — are the first to look elsewhere.

Direction is not just a strategic tool. It is a retention mechanism for the people you most want to keep.

The Misunderstood Tension

Many leaders instinctively resist giving strong direction because they fear what it implies about the people they lead.

If I tell people clearly where we are going and how we will get there, will they feel controlled? Will I send the message that I don't trust their judgment? Will I stifle the creativity and autonomy that makes our culture healthy?

These are genuine concerns, and they come from the right instincts. Leaders who have seen directive management used as a cover for micromanagement — who have watched authoritarian "clarity" crush the engagement and initiative of talented people — are right to want something different.

But this is a false tension.

Direction does not suppress engagement. It channels it.

The distinction is between direction and control. Control tells people not only where to go but exactly how to walk every step of the way. It substitutes leadership judgment for individual judgment at every decision point. It produces compliance, and over time, it produces only compliance, because people learn that their own thinking is neither needed nor welcome.

Direction tells people where the organization is going and why it matters. It establishes the destination and the purpose. And then it trusts people to bring their full capability, creativity, and judgment to the work of getting there.

Kennedy did not tell the engineers at NASA which equations to use. He told them where they were going. The how was theirs to solve — and the extraordinary ingenuity they brought to that problem was precisely what made the mission possible.

Strong direction and genuine empowerment are not opposites. They are partners. When people know clearly where the organization is headed, they can make better decisions independently. They can prioritize without constant escalation. They can innovate within a framework rather than improvising without one. Direction gives engagement something to work with.

Without it, even the most motivated people are flying without instruments.

Direction as Commitment, Not Compliance

Satya Nadella became CEO of Microsoft in 2014. He inherited a company that had spent years losing ground in mobile and cloud computing — still profitable, still large, but increasingly defined by what it was defending rather than what it was building. The internal culture had grown competitive in counterproductive ways, with employees focused on outperforming colleagues rather than outperforming competitors. Innovation had slowed. The energy in the organization had turned inward.

Nadella's response was not a restructuring plan or a cost-cutting initiative. It was a reorientation of direction.

He articulated a clear and compelling purpose: to empower every person and every organization on the planet to achieve more. He backed it with a specific strategic commitment to cloud computing and a cultural shift he described as moving from a "know-it-all" to a "learn-it-all" organization. He communicated not just where Microsoft was going, but why it mattered and what kind of organization it would need to become to get there.

What followed was not a management overhaul. It was a transformation of commitment.

Engineers who had been working on products that felt like legacy obligations began redirecting their energy toward a platform that felt like the future. Teams that had been competing internally began collaborating across divisions on shared goals. Microsoft's market value, roughly $300 billion when Nadella took over, grew more than tenfold in the decade that followed. Not because the underlying talent changed. Because the direction did.

That is directional leadership operating at scale. A clear destination, a compelling purpose, and the consistent communication that allows an organization of one hundred thousand people to move with something approaching coherence.

The lesson is not that every organization needs a visionary CEO to articulate a moon shot. The lesson is that direction — clear, honest, purposeful direction — unlocks a level of commitment that no incentive structure, no performance management system, and no amount of talent alone can replicate.

Compliance is adequate for routine work in stable conditions. But organizations that face complexity, change, and competition cannot afford adequacy. They need the kind of sustained, creative, engaged effort that only commitment produces.

And commitment follows direction.

Direction in Practice

Directional leadership is not exclusively the work of senior executives. It operates at every level of an organization — in how a department head frames a team's annual priorities, in how a project leader explains why a particular initiative matters, in how a manager connects an individual's daily work to the larger mission.

The question every leader at every level must be able to answer, clearly and convincingly, is: what are we trying to accomplish, and why does it matter?

If the answer is vague, complicated, or unconvincing, direction is not yet clear. And if direction is not yet clear at the leadership level, it will not be clear anywhere in the organization.

In my own leadership practice, our team met regularly not simply to coordinate operations but to discuss and sharpen our sense of direction. What were we actually trying to accomplish? How did our work connect to the organization's broader mission? Where were we heading, and were we heading there together? Those conversations were not administrative exercises. They were the mechanism through which direction stayed alive rather than becoming a forgotten statement in a strategic plan document.

Four disciplines are worth developing deliberately.

Clarity before communication. Direction cannot be communicated clearly if it is not yet clear in the leader's own mind. Before articulating direction to a team, effective leaders do the hard thinking necessary to distill complexity into something true and accessible. Vague direction is not better than no direction — it creates the illusion of alignment without the substance of it.

Consistency over time. Direction loses its power when it shifts frequently or when leaders' behavior contradicts what they have said. Organizations take their cues about what actually matters not from formal communications but from where leaders consistently direct their attention and energy. If the stated direction says one thing and the calendar, the budget, and the conversations in the hallway say another, people will follow the calendar.

Purpose alongside destination. Direction is most powerful when it connects where the organization is going to why the destination matters. Kennedy did not just say the United States would go to the moon. He articulated why: because the challenge was hard, because the advancement of knowledge mattered, because national capability and purpose demanded it. Purpose transforms a destination from a target into a cause.

Invitation over imposition. The most effective directional leaders do not simply announce where the organization is going. They invite others into the thinking — sharing the reasoning, acknowledging the tradeoffs, creating space for questions and honest dialogue. This is not indecisiveness. It is the recognition that people commit more deeply to directions they understand and have had the opportunity to engage with than to directions that arrive as mandates.

When Direction and Culture Work Together

Directional leadership does not operate in isolation. As we explored in Chapter 3, culture is the catalyst — the soil in which direction either takes root or doesn't.

In an organization with strong foundational trust, clear direction is received as orientation rather than prescription. People hear it and ask: how can I contribute to this? They bring their judgment, their creativity, and their initiative to the work of getting there.

In an organization with weak trust, the same clear direction lands differently. People hear it and ask: what does this mean for me? They calculate rather than commit. They wait to see whether the stated direction is real or performative, whether leadership will stay the course or shift when conditions change.

Direction and culture are not competing priorities. They are multipliers of each other. Strong direction in a strong culture produces extraordinary results. Strong direction in a weak culture produces short-term compliance and long-term disengagement. Weak direction in a strong culture produces goodwill without momentum. And weak direction in a weak culture produces exactly what you would expect.

The 3D Leadership Architecture is designed to create conditions in which all three dimensions reinforce each other. Foundational trust makes culture possible. Culture makes direction receivable. And direction gives capability something to work toward.

Signals of Directional Clarity

When direction is genuinely clear and genuinely believed, it becomes visible in how an organization operates day to day.

Decisions get made faster and with greater confidence, because people have a framework for evaluating options. Rather than escalating every ambiguous choice upward, they ask: does this move us toward where we are going? The answer is usually sufficient.

Priorities align across functions. When teams share a clear sense of direction, coordination becomes easier because there is a common reference point for resolving competing demands.

Onboarding new team members becomes more effective. When direction is clear and consistently communicated, new people orient more quickly to what the organization values and how their role connects to the larger purpose. They contribute faster because they understand sooner what they are contributing to.

Engagement deepens. People who can clearly answer the question "why does my work matter?" — and who believe the answer — bring a qualitatively different level of investment to what they do. They think about the work when they are not working. They bring ideas that were not requested.

When Direction Breaks Down

Directional failure is rarely the result of a leader who is indifferent to where the organization is going. More often, it results from leaders who know where they want to go but have not done the work of making that destination clear, compelling, and consistent enough for others to follow.

The most common failure patterns are worth naming.

Direction exists in the leader's head but not in the organization's understanding. Leaders who have thought deeply about strategy often overestimate how much of that thinking has actually been communicated. A direction that is clear to the person who developed it may be almost invisible to the people who need to act on it.

Direction is articulated once and then assumed. A single all-hands presentation or strategic planning document is not sufficient to create genuine directional clarity. Direction must be communicated repeatedly, through multiple channels, in ways that connect to the specific work that individuals and teams are doing.

Direction is stated but not demonstrated. If leaders say the organization is committed to innovation but consistently choose the safe option when it matters, people will follow behavior rather than words. Direction must be lived, not just announced.

Direction shifts too frequently. Organizations that repeatedly change stated direction teach people not to commit to it — because the current direction may not be the actual direction. Stability of direction, even amid tactical flexibility, is essential to building the kind of deep commitment that produces sustainable results.

Leadership Reflection

Consider the directional clarity in your own organization.

Direction is not a document or a presentation. It is a shared understanding, built over time through consistent communication, consistent behavior, and consistent leadership attention.

The organizations that move with genuine coherence, that accomplish things that surprise even themselves, are almost never the ones with the most talented people or the largest resources. They are the ones where people at every level can answer the same question the same way.

Where are we going?

And why does it matter?

Chapter 5 — Distributed Capability

The Leadership Capacity Dimension

Leadership is not defined solely by position.

In the late 1990s, the New Zealand All Blacks were in trouble.

By the standards of most sports organizations, "trouble" for the All Blacks would have looked like success anywhere else. They were still winning more often than not. But a team that had defined rugby excellence for a century was underperforming relative to its own standard — losing matches it shouldn't have lost, struggling with internal dysfunction, and watching rival nations close a gap that had once seemed permanent.

The response was not to hire better players. New Zealand's rugby pipeline was already among the best in the world. The response was to reimagine how leadership worked inside the team.

What emerged was a philosophy built on a simple premise: the All Blacks could not afford to concentrate leadership in a handful of senior players and the coaching staff. Not because those individuals weren't capable, but because concentration itself was the vulnerability. A team that depended on a few people to lead was fragile. A team in which leadership was genuinely distributed — where every player understood that developing those around them was as much their responsibility as performing themselves — was something else entirely.

The phrase that defined this shift was simple: better people make better All Blacks.

Not better athletes. Better people. The philosophy held that character, leadership capacity, and the genuine investment in the growth of teammates were not soft additions to a high-performance culture. They were the foundation of it. Senior players were expected to mentor those coming up. Veterans made it their business to accelerate the development of those who would eventually replace them. Leadership was treated not as a status reserved for the captain and coaches, but as a responsibility distributed across the entire squad.

The results over the following decades were historic. The All Blacks became the most successful international sports team in the history of professional rugby — and one of the most studied organizational cultures in the world, across industries far beyond sport.

The lesson they offer is not about rugby. It is about what happens when an organization stops treating leadership as a position and starts building it as a system.

Distributed capability transforms leadership from a position into a system.

The Fragility of Concentrated Leadership

Most organizations, left to develop naturally, concentrate leadership in a small number of individuals. This is understandable. Leaders earn authority through demonstrated capability. They are trusted with decisions because they have shown good judgment. Over time, the organization learns to route its most important questions and challenges through the people who have consistently provided good answers.

The problem is not that this pattern produces bad outcomes in the short term. It often produces very good ones. The problem is what it builds structurally. And what it fails to build.

An organization in which leadership is concentrated is an organization that is fragile in two distinct and important ways.

The first is departure risk. When capability and institutional knowledge live primarily in a few individuals, the departure of any one of them creates a disruption that is difficult to absorb. The problem is not the departure itself — people leave, retire, and move on. The problem is that the organization had not built the distributed capacity to absorb that loss. Leadership had been concentrated rather than cultivated across the system.

The second fragility is subtler but equally damaging: the decision bottleneck.

When decisions flow primarily through leadership, the organization's capacity to move is limited by leadership's capacity to process. In complex, fast-moving environments, this creates friction that compounds over time.

Teams wait for approvals. Initiatives stall pending direction. People with the clearest view of a problem, those closest to the work, find themselves unable to act without escalation.

There is also a signal embedded in that structure that leaders rarely intend to send. When every decision funnels upward, the implicit message to the people doing the work is that their judgment is not yet trusted. Even genuinely good intentions, a consistent pattern of centralized decision-making teaches people to stop exercising independent judgment — because they have learned, through experience, that it will be reviewed, revised, or overridden.

If leadership views team members as trusted experts in their respective areas — and if direction is genuinely clear — then those individuals should be empowered to make the decisions required to move the organization forward. The role of leadership is not to be the source of every answer. It is to develop people who can find good answers themselves.

Leadership concentrated in a few individuals creates fragile organizations. Leadership distributed across a capable, trusted, well-directed team creates something durable.

Capability Requires Culture

Distributed capability does not emerge from policy or organizational charts. It emerges from culture — specifically, from the kind of developmental culture we explored in Chapter 3. The relationship between the two dimensions runs in both directions.

Culture creates the conditions in which people feel safe enough to step into expanded responsibility. And as capability grows across the organization, it reinforces the culture — because people who have been trusted with growth model that same investment in others. Each dimension strengthens the other.

This is why the 3D Leadership Architecture treats these dimensions as interdependent rather than sequential. Weak trust makes distributed capability harder to build, because people won't accept the risk of visible growth in an environment that feels unsafe. But the reverse is equally true — an organization that talks about developmental culture while never creating real opportunities for growth eventually loses credibility. The two must move together.

Capability also requires direction. People develop most effectively when they understand not just what skills are being built, but why those skills serve the organization's larger purpose. Growth that is connected to direction feels meaningful. Growth disconnected from direction feels arbitrary.

The three dimensions reinforce each other — or, when one is missing, they undermine each other. This is what makes organizational health a system rather than a checklist.

The Coaching Culture

One of the most practical and powerful vehicles for building distributed capability is a coaching culture — and it is worth being specific about what that means, because the term is often used loosely.

A coaching culture is not primarily about formal coaching relationships or structured development programs, though both can be valuable. At its core, a coaching culture is one in which leaders at every level have internalized a particular orientation toward the people they work with: one of curiosity rather than prescription, of questions rather than answers, of genuine interest in how others are thinking rather than simply telling them what to think.

From a leadership perspective, this orientation does something that is easy to underestimate. When a leader responds to a challenge by asking questions rather than immediately providing solutions, and when their instinct is to understand before offering direction, two things happen simultaneously. The leader gains real information about how their team is thinking. And the team member experiences something important: their perspective matters. Their thinking is considered worth genuine engagement. Leadership is interested.

That experience, repeated consistently over time, is one of the most reliable drivers of engagement. People who feel that their ideas are genuinely heard and taken seriously invest more of themselves in the work.

The need for stronger leadership capability is widely recognized. Research suggests that 95% of business leaders identify becoming a better manager as an important goal for their career satisfaction — yet many organizations invest far more in strategy and operations than in developing that capability (Harris Poll/Box of Crayons, Navigating a Fractured Workplace, 2024).

From an organizational perspective, a coaching culture addresses this gap directly. When everyone in the organization — not just formal leaders — approaches their colleagues with curiosity and developmental intent, the result is an environment in which thinking improves through interaction. A well-asked question from a peer can clarify a problem that has resisted solution for weeks. People often already know the answer to their own challenges — they simply need to be led there through focused questions that help them think more clearly.

This is not a soft organizational nicety. It is a structural advantage. Organizations where people routinely help each other think more clearly make better decisions, solve problems faster, and develop capability more efficiently than those where knowledge is hoarded or people work in isolation.

Michael Bungay Stanier, in his work on coaching in organizational settings — particularly The Coaching Habit — argues that the single most useful shift a leader can make is to stay curious a little longer before offering advice or solutions. The instinct to help by answering is strong — particularly in leaders who have been rewarded throughout their careers for having good answers. But the deeper help, the kind that builds lasting capability, comes from creating the conditions in which others develop their own answers.

A coaching culture, built intentionally and modeled consistently from the top, is one of the most powerful tools available for distributing capability across an organization.

Opportunity Creates Confidence

In one department I led, leadership development often occurred through what we referred to as broadening experiences.

These opportunities allowed team members to step into responsibilities they had not previously carried. Sometimes this meant temporarily filling leadership gaps during vacancies. Other times it involved leading major initiatives, coordinating conferences, or managing projects that required collaboration across the department.

At first, stepping into these roles did not always feel natural. Confidence developed gradually. But something important happened once individuals experienced these opportunities. They began to see themselves differently. Leadership was no longer something reserved for others. They began to recognize themselves as part of the leadership capacity of the department.

That shift — from leadership is something other people do to I am part of this organization's leadership capacity — is the fundamental identity change that distributed capability requires. It cannot be achieved through training alone, or through titles, or through encouragement from above. It requires actual experience of responsibility. It requires the discovery, made personally and viscerally, that the challenge was manageable and the growth was real.

Opportunity creates confidence. Not the other way around.

This sequencing matters for leaders who are building distributed capability. The instinct is often to wait until someone is fully ready before expanding their responsibility — to develop confidence first and then offer opportunity. But confidence of the kind that changes how people see themselves does not precede challenge. It follows it. The role of leadership is to create the conditions in which people can step into experiences that are stretching but survivable, supported but genuinely challenging.

Learning Through Responsibility

When individuals stepped into broader roles, they worked diligently to develop the skills required to succeed. They sought advice from colleagues. They asked questions of supervisors and leaders. They surrounded themselves with people who could provide feedback and guidance.

The environment around them supported that growth.

Team members were eager to help one another succeed. Leadership provided mentorship, consultation, and perspective when challenges emerged. Responsibility became a learning opportunity rather than a test. People were encouraged to grow rather than judged for inexperience.

This environment did not appear automatically. It was built — through consistent leadership behavior that modeled curiosity over judgment, through a culture that treated honest questions as signs of strength rather than weakness, and through the clear signal, sent repeatedly over time, that growth was something the organization valued and invested in.

The result was an accelerating cycle. As more people stepped into expanded responsibility and succeeded, the organization's collective confidence in its own distributed capability grew. The pool of people willing to step forward expanded. The range of challenges the organization could absorb without depending on a small number of individuals widened.

Distributed capability, once genuinely established, tends to compound.

Mentorship Strengthens Capability

Mentorship played an important role in this process — particularly as individuals stepped into leadership responsibilities that involved supervising others for the first time.

New supervisors face a specific and underappreciated challenge. The skills that made them effective individual contributors are not the same skills required to develop and support a team. The transition is not automatic. And in organizations that promote people into supervision without meaningful support, the resulting struggles often damage both the new leader and the people they are trying to lead.

Intentional mentorship changes this.

When experienced leaders invest time and genuine attention in those navigating new leadership responsibilities — sharing advice, offering consultation on specific challenges, helping emerging leaders understand the difference between what they are seeing and what is actually happening — the development curve accelerates significantly. Common pitfalls are avoided not because the new leader was warned away from them generically, but because someone with relevant experience helped them recognize the specific situation they faced.

Mentorship also communicates organizational values in the most direct way possible: through the behavior of leaders who are willing to invest their own time and attention in someone else's growth. When emerging leaders experience that investment, they internalize not just the practical guidance but the implicit message — that developing others is what leaders here do. That norm, modeled and then replicated, is how a coaching culture becomes self-sustaining.

Career development and leadership development are not separate tracks in a healthy organization. They are woven together — supported by mentors who help individuals understand not only how to grow in their current role but how their growth connects to a larger professional trajectory. When people can see a path forward and believe that the organization is genuinely invested in helping them walk it, engagement deepens in ways that no compensation structure can fully replicate.

Capability Strengthens the System

As leadership capacity expanded across the department, something noticeable began to occur.

More people stepped forward to solve problems. Initiatives gained momentum because responsibility was shared rather than centralized. New ideas emerged from multiple places within the organization. Individuals began approaching challenges with a simple mindset: what do we need to do for the organization to succeed?

That shift represented something deeper than skill development. It reflected ownership.

When individuals begin thinking about the success of the entire organization — rather than only their assigned roles — leadership capacity has truly become distributed.

This is the destination that the 3D Leadership Architecture points toward in this dimension. Not a department full of people who are competent at their jobs, though that matters. Not a succession plan that identifies a small number of high-potential individuals for eventual promotion, though that has value. But an organization where the default instinct is to ask what we need to do — rather than whose responsibility it is — and where that instinct has become the way people actually think and act.

That organization is not fragile. It does not depend on any single individual. It does not require every decision to be made at the top. It has built, through intentional investment over time, the distributed leadership capacity to adapt, absorb difficulty, and continue moving forward even when circumstances change.

This is what the All Blacks understood. This is what the most consistently high-performing organizations in every sector have built, each in their own way.

Leadership is not a position. It is a system.

And systems, unlike individuals, do not leave.

Leadership Reflection

Consider the distribution of leadership capability in your own organization.

Distributed capability is not built in a single initiative or through a single program. It is built through the accumulation of small decisions: to offer an opportunity rather than wait for readiness, to ask a question rather than provide an answer, to invest an hour in someone's development rather than solve their problem for them.

Those decisions, made consistently over time, transform an organization from one that depends on its leaders to one that develops them — at every level, in every role, as a natural expression of how the work gets done.

Leadership concentrated at the top is efficient in the short term and fragile in the long term. Leadership distributed across the system is harder to build and nearly impossible to break.

PART III
Strengthening the Architecture

Chapter 6 — When the Architecture Breaks Down

When organizations begin struggling, leaders often search for explanations.

The first assumption is usually people.

Perhaps the team lacks talent. Perhaps individuals are not working hard enough. Perhaps a few difficult personalities are disrupting progress.

If those explanations do not fully account for the problem, attention often shifts to resources. Maybe the organization needs more funding. More staff. More time. More tools.

Occasionally these explanations are accurate.

But more often, the real issue lies elsewhere.

The issue is structural.

A Familiar Pattern

Consider a scenario that plays out in organizations more often than most leaders would care to admit.

A supervisor sets a specific directive, precise, detailed, non-negotiable in their mind. A team member receives the directive, encounters real-world constraints that make the exact specification unworkable, and makes a reasonable judgment call to deliver the best available outcome given what is actually possible. The result is good work. It solves the underlying problem. But it does not match what the supervisor originally specified.

The supervisor's response is to identify the employee as the problem.

Not the directive. Not the constraints. Not the gap between what was asked and what was achievable. The person.

This pattern is recognizable to almost anyone who has spent time inside organizations. And it illustrates precisely the diagnostic failure at the heart of this chapter. The supervisor is not examining the structure: the clarity of the expectation, the reality of the constraints, the degree to which the directive allowed for professional judgment. The supervisor is examining the person. And because the person is visible and the structure is not, the person becomes the answer to a question that should have been asked differently.

When the architecture of an organization weakens, the symptoms often appear in the behavior of people and the pressure on resources. But those symptoms are rarely the root cause.

The real question is almost always structural: what in the design of this organization is producing this outcome?

The Dimensions Reinforce Each Other — In Both Directions

Before exploring how the architecture breaks down, it is worth understanding how it builds up — because the same interdependence that makes dysfunction spread is what makes health compound.

When Directional Leadership is strong, it does more than align effort. It gives the Developmental Culture something to grow toward. People invest more deeply in their own development when they can see clearly how that development serves a larger purpose. And when capability expands across the organization, direction becomes easier to execute because more people are equipped to carry it.

When Developmental Culture is strong, it creates the safety that Distributed Capability requires. People step into expanded responsibility only in environments where growth is genuinely supported. And as people develop through those experiences, they reinforce the culture by modeling the investment in others that was once modeled for them.

When Distributed Capability is strong, it takes pressure off directional leadership and frees culture to breathe. Organizations that are not bottlenecked at the top move faster, adapt more readily, and sustain momentum through disruption that would stall a more concentrated structure.

And underlying all three, Foundational Trust either amplifies or undermines everything. In an environment of strong trust, each dimension builds on the others. In an environment of thin trust, each dimension struggles to take hold regardless of how well it is designed on paper.

The architecture, when healthy, is self-reinforcing. Each dimension growing strengthens the others. This is what organizational health feels like from the inside — not the absence of difficulty, but the presence of a system that meets difficulty with increasing rather than decreasing capacity.

The reverse is equally true. When one dimension weakens, the others come under strain. Understanding that pattern is what allows leaders to diagnose problems accurately rather than react to symptoms.

Within the 3D Leadership Architecture, strain tends to appear when one of the structural dimensions weakens relative to the others. When this happens, organizations often fall into predictable patterns.

Direction Without Culture

In some organizations, direction remains strong while culture begins to weaken.

Leaders set clear goals. Strategy is defined. Expectations are communicated. From the outside, the organization may appear decisive and productive.

But beneath the surface, trust is thin.

People receive direction clearly enough, but they do not feel safe enough to push back when the direction is flawed, or to surface the information that might improve it. Disagreement becomes cautious rather than constructive. Communication narrows to what is safe rather than what is true. People comply with decisions but no longer feel comfortable contributing ideas freely.

This is the pattern that the scenario at the opening of this chapter represents. Direction was present, specific and clear. But the culture surrounding it did not create enough safety for honest dialogue about what was actually achievable. The gap between directive and reality could not be surfaced without risk. So it wasn't surfaced. It was managed privately. And when the outcome reflected that gap, the culture's absence made blame the available response.

Results may still appear strong for a time. But performance becomes increasingly dependent on authority and pressure rather than engagement. Over time, energy fades. Initiative declines. The organization continues moving forward — but under growing strain.

The long-term cost of direction without culture is not dramatic collapse. It is the gradual erosion of the discretionary effort that separates adequate performance from excellent performance. People do what is asked. They stop doing more.

Culture Without Direction

In other organizations, culture remains positive while direction becomes unclear.

Relationships are strong. People enjoy working together. Communication flows easily across teams. The environment is warm, trusting, and genuinely supportive of the people within it.

Yet priorities begin to drift.

Strategy feels uncertain. Initiatives multiply without clear alignment. Energy disperses across too many efforts, each of them reasonable in isolation, none of them building toward a coherent destination. People remain busy and well-intentioned, but progress becomes uneven.

This pattern is in some ways the most painful, because the goodwill is real and the people are genuinely invested. The problem is not motivation or trust or the quality of the relationships. The problem is that all of that energy has no clear channel. Without direction, even a healthy culture struggles to maintain momentum.

The organization becomes comfortable — but unfocused.

Over time, the lack of visible progress begins to erode the culture itself. People who care about meaningful work eventually become frustrated when they cannot see how their effort is contributing to something larger. The warmth of the culture provides less and less compensation for the absence of a shared sense of purpose. Engagement, which felt strong when the culture was building, begins to hollow out.

Direction is what gives culture somewhere to go. Without it, even the healthiest culture eventually loses its energy.

Leadership Without Capability

A third pattern appears when direction and culture remain relatively strong, but leadership capacity has not been distributed throughout the organization.

In these environments, leaders set clear direction and maintain positive working relationships. People understand the mission. Trust exists. The culture supports honest communication and genuine engagement.

But execution begins to stall.

Too many decisions require attention from a small number of leaders. Work accumulates around key individuals. Every significant question flows upward, not because people lack judgment, but because the organization has not yet built the structures and trust required for that judgment to be exercised independently.

Growth places increasing pressure on the same limited group of decision-makers. The people who are capable of solving problems wait for permission to solve them. The people who hold authority become the bottleneck for an organization that is otherwise ready to move.

The organization may feel healthy in spirit, but it is fragile in structure. Without broader leadership capability throughout the system, momentum becomes difficult to sustain — and the departure of any one of the concentrated leaders creates a disruption the organization is not designed to absorb.

This pattern often develops not through neglect but through success. Organizations that have grown around strong individual leaders frequently arrive here. The leaders are genuinely excellent. The problem is not their capability. It is that their capability was never systematically distributed.

WHEN THE SYSTEM IS OUT OF BALANCE

When one dimension weakens, the system breaks in predictable ways.

Weak Directional Leadership	Weak Developmental Culture	Weak Distributed Capability
Looks like: • Activity without alignment • Constant reprioritization • Decisions disconnected from purpose • Confusion about what matters	**Looks like:** • Silence in meetings • Hesitation to speak up • Feedback avoided • Cautious or guarded communication	**Looks like:** • Decisions bottleneck at the top • Leaders overloaded • Teams wait instead of act • Ownership stays at the top
Results in: ▸ Drift and disengagement	**Results in:** ▸ Artificial harmony and hidden dysfunction	**Results in:** ▸ Dependence and slowdown

Diagnosing the Architecture

Recognizing these patterns allows leaders to diagnose problems more accurately.

Instead of immediately assuming the issue lies with individuals or resources, leaders can step back and examine the structure of the organization itself. The questions are straightforward, but they require honesty to answer well.

Is direction genuinely clear — not just communicated, but understood and believed at every level of the organization? Does the culture reinforce trust and psychological safety, or does it reward compliance and punish candor? Is leadership capacity distributed broadly enough to support growth and absorb disruption, or is the organization dependent on a small number of individuals whose departure would destabilize it?

When one dimension weakens relative to the others, the architecture of the organization begins to tilt. From the outside, the organization may still appear stable. But internally, strain increases as one pillar begins carrying more weight than the structure was designed to support.

The issue is rarely individual performance. It is architectural imbalance.

These questions shift the conversation from blame to design. They encourage leaders to strengthen the architecture rather than simply react to symptoms. That shift — from what is wrong with the people to what is wrong with the structure — is one of the most important moves an organizational leader can make.

It is also, in most organizational cultures, one of the harder ones. Blaming structure requires leaders to examine their own design choices. Blaming people is easier and carries less personal accountability. The leader who is willing to look at the architecture honestly, including the parts they built, is the leader who can actually fix what is broken.

Design Determines Strength

Organizations rarely fail because people suddenly lose their ability to perform.

More often, the structure surrounding those people begins to weaken. When trust erodes, culture becomes fragile. When direction is unclear, effort disperses. When capability is concentrated in too few individuals, progress slows under the weight of responsibility.

These are not failures of individual effort. They are failures of design — and they are correctable through design.

Healthy organizations avoid these patterns not by accident but through intentional and ongoing attention to the architecture itself. They do not assume that a structure that worked last year will work next year without maintenance. They diagnose early, before imbalance becomes visible in performance data. They ask the architectural questions regularly, not just in moments of crisis.

And critically, they strengthen direction, culture, and capability simultaneously, recognizing that each dimension both depends on and reinforces the others.

When these dimensions align on a foundation of trust, organizations gain something that cannot be purchased, mandated, or manufactured in a single initiative.

They gain resilience.

Resilience is not the absence of difficulty. It is the capacity to meet difficulty without structural collapse — to absorb disruption, leadership transition, resource pressure, and unexpected challenge without losing the coherence and momentum that healthy architecture provides. Resilient organizations have seen hard things and moved through them. They have lost key people and developed others to fill the gap. They have faced unclear terrain and found their direction again because the culture supported honest navigation.

The architecture itself begins supporting performance rather than straining against it. And when the architecture is strong, organizations develop the capacity to carry pressure without being broken by it.

The most resilient organizations do not simply survive pressure. They reframe it.

Pressure, in a healthy organization, is not a sign that something is wrong. It is a sign that the work matters — that the stakes are real, that people are invested, and that what this organization does is worth doing under difficult conditions. The highest-performing teams in every field understand this intuitively. Pressure is not the enemy of excellence. It is often the condition that produces it.

Kirby Smart, head football coach at the University of Georgia, captured this idea simply and memorably: pressure is a privilege. The teams that feel it most are the ones competing for something worth having. The organizations that carry it longest are the ones that have built something worth protecting.

That reframe is available to any organization willing to build the architecture that makes it possible. When trust runs deep, when culture is genuinely developmental, when direction is clear and capability is broadly distributed — pressure becomes something an organization can carry without being broken by it.

That is not a burden. That is a privilege.

Leadership Reflection

When organizations struggle, leaders often focus first on people or resources. But structural problems are often the real cause.

Consider your own organization.

Strengthening the architecture, rather than reacting to symptoms, is often the most effective path forward. It requires leaders to look honestly at what they have built, acknowledge where the structure is serving the organization and where it is not, and make the deliberate design choices that move the system toward health.

The goal is not a perfect organization. It is a resilient one — capable of meeting pressure with capacity rather than collapse, and of growing stronger, over time, through the very challenges that would destabilize a structure built on thinner foundations.

Chapter 7 — Signals of Organizational Health

ASSESSING THE SYSTEM

Where are we strong? Where are we vulnerable?

Directional Leadership	Developmental Culture	Distributed Capability
• Are priorities clear and consistent?	• Do people speak openly under pressure?	• Are leaders actively developing others?
• Do people understand what matters most?	• Is feedback expected and safe?	• Are decisions made at the right level?
• Are decisions aligned to direction?	• Is tension addressed constructively?	• Do people take ownership beyond their role?
• Is purpose clearly connected to the work?	• Do people feel safe contributing ideas?	• Is leadership growing across the organization?

Healthy organizations rarely announce themselves through reports or dashboards.

They reveal themselves through the energy of everyday work.

What You Notice When You Walk In

Every experienced leader knows the feeling.

You walk into an organization — a department, a team, a building — and within minutes, sometimes seconds, you sense something about how the place actually functions. Not from the data. Not from the org chart. From the atmosphere.

In some environments, the air feels heavy. People move through their work with their heads down. Hallways are quiet in a way that doesn't feel peaceful — it feels guarded. Meetings start on time, cover the agenda, and end without much having been said. When you ask someone how things are going, the answer is brief and careful.

In others, something is unmistakably different. People are talking — not just in scheduled meetings but in doorways, in common spaces, across functions. There is a quality to the energy that is hard to name precisely but impossible to miss. Problems are being worked on. Ideas are moving. Someone is laughing. The place feels alive.

That difference is not personality. It is not luck. It is not the result of hiring particularly enthusiastic people.

It is the visible expression of a healthy organizational architecture.

Gallup's ongoing State of the Global Workplace research has confirmed what most experienced leaders already sense: employees who feel engaged and connected to their organization are significantly more likely to take initiative, collaborate, and contribute ideas. Engagement is not a mood. It is a structural outcome — the product of an environment that has been designed, intentionally or accidentally, to bring out the best in the people within it.

When foundational trust is strong and the three dimensions of the 3D Leadership Architecture align, organizations begin to exhibit recognizable signals. These signals are not found in quarterly reports or annual reviews. They are found in the texture of daily work — in who speaks up in meetings, in how problems get solved, in whether the energy of the building on a Monday morning feels like possibility or obligation.

Three signals appear consistently.

Energy. Alignment. Momentum.

Energy

Energy is often the first visible indicator of organizational health — and the first to disappear when health begins to weaken.

In a healthy organization, energy expresses itself in specific and observable ways. People volunteer for projects before they are assigned. They offer ideas in meetings without being prompted. They ask questions that go beyond their immediate responsibilities because they are genuinely curious about the larger picture. When a problem surfaces, someone moves toward it rather than waiting to see whose job it technically is.

Conversation flows naturally across teams and across levels of the hierarchy. Colleagues stop by one another's offices — not because a process requires it, but because the exchange of thinking feels valuable and the relationships make it easy. The informal connections that happen in common spaces and hallways carry real organizational work. Problems get identified and partially solved before they ever reach a formal meeting.

Energy does not mean constant enthusiasm or the performance of positivity. It means something quieter and more durable: people feel safe enough to participate fully. They bring their actual thinking to the work rather than a carefully managed version of it. They engage because the environment has taught them that engagement is welcome and worthwhile.

When I think about the healthiest environments I have experienced, the atmosphere sometimes reminds me of the R.E.M. song "Shiny Happy People." Not because everything was perfect. Organizations with genuine energy still face difficulty, disagreement, and hard days. But because people were engaged. They were genuinely positive about the work — not performed positivity, but the real kind that comes from believing in what you are doing and trusting the people you are doing it with. They collaborated naturally. There was a shared sense that something meaningful was being built together.

That feeling was not accidental. It was the product of an architecture that had been built to support it.

When trust weakens, energy is often the first signal to fade. The change is rarely dramatic. Doors close — literally. Participation declines in meetings. People begin conserving effort rather than offering initiative, redirecting energy that once went into the work into self-protection instead. The informal conversations in the hallway become quieter and then stop altogether.

Leaders who notice this shift early have a significant advantage. By the time energy loss shows up in performance metrics, it has usually been declining for a long time.

Alignment

Alignment is the second signal — and it is often misunderstood.

Alignment does not mean agreement. It does not mean that everyone in the organization holds the same opinion, supports every decision enthusiastically, or refrains from vigorous debate. In fact, an organization where disagreement never surfaces is almost certainly not aligned — it is silenced, which is a very different condition with very different consequences.

Genuine alignment means that people share a clear understanding of where the organization is going and why it matters, and that this shared understanding is strong enough to hold the team together even through disagreement about how to get there.

In an aligned organization, people may debate ideas energetically during discussion. Different perspectives are welcomed and genuinely considered. But once a decision is made, the organization moves forward together. The debate was real, and now the commitment is real. People carry the decision forward not because they were ordered to but because they understood the reasoning and trust the process.

Priorities are clear across levels and functions. When individuals in different parts of the organization are asked what the team's most important current work is, their answers are recognizably consistent. Work connects logically to larger goals in ways that people can actually articulate — not in the language of a strategic plan document, but in their own words, from genuine understanding.

Individuals understand why their efforts matter. This is perhaps the most important dimension of alignment, and the most frequently neglected. It is not enough for people to know what they are supposed to do. They need to understand how that work connects to something larger than the task itself. When that connection is clear, discretionary effort follows naturally. When it is not, people do what is required and stop there.

Without alignment, organizations become busy but fragmented. Teams work hard and with genuine intention, yet progress feels uneven because energy is dispersed across competing priorities that were never clearly reconciled. The effort is real. The coherence is missing.

Momentum

Momentum is the third signal — and in some ways the most powerful, because it is what the other two signals produce when they are working together.

Momentum feels different from simple activity. Busy organizations expend effort. Healthy organizations convert effort into forward movement. The distinction is not subtle once you have experienced both. In an organization with genuine momentum, work builds on itself. Progress from last week creates the foundation for this week. Solutions developed for one challenge become templates for the next. The organization is learning as it moves, and the learning accelerates the movement.

Projects advance without constant intervention from senior leaders. Teams anticipate challenges and address them before those challenges become crises. When problems arise — and they always do — the response is quick and competent because the distributed capability we explored in Chapter 5 means that the people closest to the problem are equipped to address it.

Ideas connect to and build upon previous successes rather than starting from scratch each time. Institutional memory is alive and accessible because the culture supports honest conversation about what has worked and what has not. Innovation is not sporadic — it is a natural product of a system that creates space for it consistently.

Momentum signals that the underlying architecture of the organization is functioning well. It is not the product of a single initiative or a particularly strong quarter. It is the product of direction, culture, and capability reinforcing each other over time — the architecture operating as it was designed to.

When momentum is present, the organization has a quality that is difficult to manufacture from the outside and nearly impossible to fake from the inside. People feel it. They know they are part of something that is moving. And that feeling — of being part of something that is genuinely going somewhere — is one of the most powerful drivers of sustained engagement that any organization can offer.

Reading the Signals

These three signals — energy, alignment, and momentum — give leaders a practical, everyday diagnostic for organizational health. They do not require a formal process to apply. They require attention and honesty.

When energy is present, people are participating fully and the environment feels alive. When alignment is present, effort is coherent and purpose is clear. When momentum is present, the system itself is doing real work, and progress is happening not just because people are pushing hard but because the architecture is supporting the movement.

When all three signals appear consistently, leaders can be confident that the organizational structure is functioning well. The foundation of trust is holding. The three dimensions are reinforcing each other. The system is healthy.

When the signals begin to fade, when energy declines, when alignment fragments, when momentum stalls, it is rarely a sudden failure. It is an early indication that one of the structural dimensions requires attention. The signal that fades first often points toward the dimension that is weakening. Declining energy frequently signals a culture problem. Fragmenting alignment frequently signals a direction problem. Stalling momentum frequently signals a capability problem.

These are not rigid diagnoses. Any dimension can affect any signal. But as a starting point for inquiry, the pattern holds often enough to be useful.

Reading these signals accurately and responding to them early is one of the most important practices of organizational leadership. It requires leaders to pay attention not just to what the organization is producing, but to how it feels to work within it: to notice the energy in the room, the quality of conversation, and whether people are leaning in or quietly pulling back.

Healthy organizations pay attention to these signals. They recognize that performance is not simply the result of effort. It is the result of a healthy system working together. And when the architecture is strong, the atmosphere of the organization reflects it — in the energy of the people, in the coherence of their effort, and in the sense of forward movement that makes the work feel like it is going somewhere worth going.

Leadership Reflection

The following questions serve as a practical diagnostic of your organization's health. Answer them honestly, not based on your best days, but based on your typical ones.

If the honest answers to most of these questions are encouraging, your organization is likely experiencing the signals of health, and the architecture beneath those signals is doing its work.

If the answers reveal gaps, if the meeting is quiet, if alignment is fragile, if momentum has stalled, those gaps are worth taking seriously. Not as judgments of the people in the organization, but as signals about the structure surrounding them.

The signals are always telling you something. The question is whether you are paying attention.

Chapter 8 — Designing Healthy Organizations

Healthy organizations are not built through mission statements or strategic plans alone.

They are built through leadership behavior.

Small decisions. Everyday interactions. Consistent signals that shape how people experience the organization from the inside.

Throughout this book we have explored the architecture that makes organizational health possible: the foundational trust that holds everything together, and the three dimensions of Directional Leadership, Developmental Culture, and Distributed Capability that determine whether that trust deepens into something durable and high-performing or slowly erodes under the weight of misalignment and neglect.

The architecture is real. But architecture does not build itself.

Leaders often ask where organizational health begins. The answer is simpler than many expect.

It begins with how leaders show up.

Monday Morning Leadership

If a leader asked me where to begin improving organizational health, my advice would be simple.

Start Monday morning.

Walk into the workplace with intention. Not with an agenda or a directive or a message to deliver. With genuine presence — the kind that communicates, before a single word is spoken, that the people in this organization matter to the person leading it.

Greet people warmly. Speak kindly. Show genuine interest in the individuals who make the organization function every day. Ask how they are doing and mean it. Make eye contact. Remember what someone mentioned last week about a project they were wrestling with, and ask how it turned out.

If someone recently completed a project or handled a challenge well, acknowledge it. Not in a formal recognition ceremony, but in the hallway, in the moment, in the way that makes clear you were paying attention. Express appreciation in the specific, personal way that tells someone their contribution was actually seen rather than generically noted.

These actions may seem small. They are not. They are signals. And organizations are deeply attuned to the signals their leaders send.

Every interaction communicates something about the environment leaders are creating. Do people feel seen? Do they feel respected? Do they feel that their contributions matter and that leadership is genuinely interested in them as people, not just as functions? The accumulated answers to those questions, delivered through thousands of small interactions over months and years, are the materials from which culture is actually made.

Trust grows through these signals. Not through policy announcements or values statements, but through the consistent, repeated experience of being treated with genuine regard by the people in authority.

Connection Builds Trust

Some leaders dismiss informal conversation as unproductive. Small talk, they argue, distracts from real work. There is always something more pressing to address, always a meeting to prepare for, always a decision waiting.

In reality, connection is often the foundation of effective work — and the investment of a few minutes of genuine human attention pays returns that no efficiency initiative can replicate.

Talking with people — not simply talking to them — creates the relationships that allow collaboration to flourish. It builds familiarity. It builds understanding. It builds the kind of trust that allows difficult conversations to happen directly rather than around the edges, that allows people to surface problems early rather than managing them privately, that allows an organization to function with the honest communication that high performance requires.

When individuals feel genuinely connected to their colleagues and to their leaders, they are far more willing to engage, contribute ideas, take initiative, and address challenges openly. The psychological safety that research has identified as the foundation of high-performing teams is built, in large part, through exactly these informal interactions — the accumulated experience of being heard, respected, and taken seriously by the people around you.

These interactions are not distractions from productivity. They are investments in it. The leader who spends ten minutes in genuine conversation with a team member is not losing ten minutes. They are building the relational foundation that makes the next month of collaborative work more effective.

Leadership as Daily Practice

Designing healthy organizations does not require perfect conditions or a complete organizational overhaul before work can begin. It requires something both simpler and harder: consistent leadership behavior, practiced day after day, until that behavior becomes the signal the organization trusts.

Healthy organizations are built on trust and strengthened through clear direction, developmental culture, and distributed capability.

Leaders reinforce direction by communicating purpose clearly and repeatedly, not just in all-hands meetings but in the hallway conversations, in the way they frame decisions, and in the questions they ask that reveal what they actually care about. Direction is communicated less through formal channels than through the consistent evidence of where a leader's attention goes.

They reinforce culture by modeling respect, transparency, and constructive dialogue. Culture follows the leader's example more faithfully than it follows any stated value. When a leader handles a difficult conversation with honesty and care, they teach the organization how difficult conversations are handled. When they respond to a mistake with curiosity rather than blame, they teach the organization what it means to make a mistake here.

They reinforce capability by encouraging growth, providing mentorship, and trusting people with responsibility before those people feel fully ready — because full readiness is usually a signal that the opportunity came too late.

These actions compound over time. What begins as a simple interaction becomes a pattern. A pattern becomes an expectation. An expectation becomes culture. And culture, once genuinely established, begins reinforcing the architecture itself. It produces new leaders, new ideas, and new capacity — without requiring the same constant investment that built it.

That is what organizational health, fully realized, actually looks like. Not a system that requires constant maintenance from the top, but one that generates its own momentum because the people within it have made those values their own and carry them forward.

Strengthening the Three Dimensions

Leaders strengthen organizational health by intentionally reinforcing the three dimensions of the 3D Leadership Architecture — not as a periodic exercise but as the ongoing discipline of leadership itself.

Directional Leadership ensures people understand where the organization is going and why their work matters. It is reinforced every time a leader connects a daily decision to the larger purpose, every time they explain the reasoning behind a direction rather than simply issuing it, every time they create space for questions that deepen rather than merely communicate understanding.

Developmental Culture creates an environment where individuals feel safe engaging fully — with their work, with their colleagues, and with the challenges the organization faces. It is reinforced every time a leader responds to honesty with appreciation rather than defensiveness, every time they celebrate a good question as readily as a good answer, every time they treat a mistake as information rather than indictment.

Distributed Capability expands leadership capacity throughout the organization, ensuring that initiative, responsibility, and growth exist at every level rather than concentrating at the top. It is reinforced every time a leader offers an opportunity instead of an assignment, asks a coaching question instead of providing a solution, and trusts a team member with a decision that could have been made higher up the organization.

When these dimensions operate together on a foundation of trust, organizations become remarkably resilient. Pressure clarifies rather than destabilizes. Problems become opportunities for collaboration rather than sources of blame. Momentum begins to build naturally — not because leadership is pushing harder, but because the architecture is working.

THE LEADERSHIP LEVERS

How leaders actively shape direction, culture, and capability

Directional Leadership	Developmental Culture	Distributed Capability
• Clearly define and reinforce priorities	• Model behavior under pressure	• Actively develop leaders at all levels
• Consistently communicate what matters most	• Make feedback expected and safe	• Empower decision-making at all levels
• Align decisions to the stated direction	• Address tension directly and constructively	• Create shared ownership

Trust is reinforced through consistency.

A Simple Organizational Health Diagnostic

Leaders who want to strengthen organizational health can begin by asking a few honest questions — not the answers they hope are true, but the answers they actually observe in the everyday life of the organization.

The full 3D Leadership Diagnostic in Appendix B offers twenty structured questions across all four elements of the architecture, with scoring and interpretation.

A digital version with automatic scoring is also available at 3dleadershipcoaching.com/3d_leadership_diagnostic

Organizations rarely struggle equally in all areas. More often, one weakened dimension begins to strain the others, and that strain shows up first not in performance data but in the signals we explored in Chapter 7. Energy fades before numbers decline. Alignment fragments before results suffer. Momentum stalls before the quarterly report reflects it.

Recognizing where the structure needs strengthening, and responding before the symptoms become visible in performance, is the practice that separates leaders who build healthy organizations from those who manage troubled ones.

The Interdependent Equations in Appendix C offer a structural lens for that diagnosis — mapping what each combination of dimensions produces, and where to look when the architecture is under strain.

Leadership Shapes the Environment

Organizations are living systems shaped by the behavior of their leaders.

Every decision sends a signal. Every conversation reinforces or weakens trust. Every interaction contributes to the environment people experience each day — the environment that either draws out their best or gradually teaches them to hold it back.

Healthy organizations emerge when leaders consistently model the behaviors they hope to see throughout the system. Trust. Respect. Engagement. Ownership. When leaders demonstrate these behaviors with enough consistency that they become the organizational norm, something profound happens. Others follow — not because they were told to, but because the environment makes those behaviors feel natural and safe.

Culture strengthens. Capability grows. Direction becomes easier to maintain because people believe in where they are going and trust the people leading them there.

Designing What Endures

Organizational health is not about creating a moment of success. It is about building an environment where success can continue — where the conditions that produced good outcomes this year are still present and still functional next year, not because nothing has changed, but because the architecture is strong enough to absorb change without losing its coherence.

Healthy organizations adapt more easily to difficulty. They solve problems more quickly because the people closest to those problems are trusted and equipped to address them. They develop new leaders because the culture treats development as a shared responsibility. They sustain engagement because people find meaning in the work and trust in the environment — and that combination is more durable than any incentive structure.

Foundational trust supports the structure. Directional leadership provides clarity. Developmental culture sustains engagement. Distributed capability strengthens the entire system.

When these elements align, organizations do more than perform.

They flourish.

Performance can exist without health. Organizations can produce results through pressure and authority and the sheer force of capable individuals working very hard. But the cost is high and the durability is low. The people doing that work feel it. And eventually they make different choices.

Healthy organizations are the ones that sustain performance — not by eliminating pressure, but by building the architecture that allows people to carry it well.

And leaders discover, usually through experience rather than instruction, that the work of building healthy organizations is not as complicated as it sometimes appears.

It begins with how they show up each day.

Not with a grand announcement. Not with a strategic planning offsite or a new initiative. But with the quiet consistency of leadership practiced over time — present, intentional, and genuinely invested in the people and the work.

A conversation handled with respect strengthens trust.

A leader who listens openly strengthens culture.

A decision explained clearly strengthens direction.

A mentor who invests in someone's growth strengthens capability.

None of these moments appear dramatic on their own. Each of them is easy to skip when the calendar is full and the pressure is high. But leadership rarely transforms organizations through dramatic moments. It transforms them through the accumulation of small ones — through the consistency of showing up the same way, day after day, until people believe that the way you show up is the way this organization actually works.

Over time, those small decisions shape the environment people experience every day.

Trust deepens. Culture strengthens. Capability expands. Direction becomes clearer. And slowly, almost quietly, the architecture of the organization becomes something that can carry weight without breaking — something resilient, something worth being part of, something that outlasts any individual leader because it was never dependent on any individual leader alone.

Healthy organizations are not accidental.

They are built — interaction by interaction, decision by decision, day by day.

And every leader, at every level, has the opportunity to help build one.

Appendix A — The 3D Leadership Framework

Healthy organizations do not emerge by accident. They are the result of intentional leadership design.

At the center of healthy organizations lies a simple truth:

Performance is not the same as health.

Organizations can produce results for a time while internal systems quietly weaken. Sustainable performance emerges when leaders intentionally strengthen the underlying architecture of the organization.

That architecture is built on foundational trust and strengthened through three structural dimensions.

Foundational Trust

The foundation upon which everything rests.

Trust exists when people believe leadership behavior is consistent, communication is transparent, expectations are fair, and accountability is predictable.

Without trust, culture strains and engagement fades.

With trust, pressure clarifies rather than destabilizes.

Directional Leadership

Clarity about where the organization is going and how it will operate along the way.

Directional leadership connects daily work to meaningful purpose and ensures teams move forward together rather than in fragmented efforts.

Compliance completes tasks. Commitment moves organizations forward.

Direction does not suppress engagement. It channels it.

Developmental Culture

The environment in which people work together.

Healthy cultures reinforce belonging, encourage constructive disagreement, and create psychological safety for people to contribute fully.

Culture is not what organizations say they value. It is how people behave when pressure appears.

Culture sets the breakfast table and invites Strategy to sit down.

Distributed Capability

Leadership capacity developed throughout the organization.

Distributed capability ensures that initiative, decision-making, and growth are not concentrated in a small number of individuals but cultivated across the entire system.

Leadership concentrated in a few individuals creates fragile organizations.

Distributed capability transforms leadership from a position into a system.

Signals of Organizational Health

When the architecture is functioning well, three signals appear consistently.

Energy — People participate fully. Initiative is visible. Informal connection flows naturally. Engagement is genuine rather than performed.

Alignment — Individuals understand how their work connects to the larger purpose. Debate is honest and decisions are carried forward with shared commitment.

Momentum — Progress builds on itself. Problems are addressed before they become crises. The architecture is doing real work.

The 3D Leadership Architecture is a diagnostic and design tool. It helps leaders identify where organizational health is strong, where it is weakening, and what intentional action will strengthen it.

Use this framework as both a diagnostic and a design tool: to identify where your organization's architecture is strong, where it needs attention, and where intentional leadership can make the greatest difference.

Appendix B — The 3D Leadership Diagnostic

The 3D Leadership Diagnostic is designed to give you an honest picture of your organization's current health — where the architecture is strong, where it is under strain, and where intentional attention will produce the greatest return.

The assessment takes less than ten minutes to complete. It is most useful when answered honestly — not based on your best days or your aspirations for the organization, but based on what you actually observe in everyday organizational life.

Rate each statement on a scale of 1 to 5:

1 (Strongly Disagree) · 2 (Disagree) · 3 (Neutral)

4 (Agree) · 5 (Strongly Agree)

Complete all twenty statements before reviewing your scores.

Complete all twenty statements before reviewing your scores.

Take the diagnostic online — scan the code or visit:

3dleadershipcoaching.com/3d_leadership_diagnostic

Section 1 — Foundational Trust

1. Leaders in this organization communicate openly and honestly, even when the news is difficult.

   1   2   3   4   5

2. People in this organization feel safe expressing disagreement or raising concerns without fear of negative consequences.

1   2   3   4   5

3. Accountability in this organization is applied consistently — the same expectations apply to everyone regardless of position.

1   2   3   4   5

4. When decisions are made, leadership explains the reasoning rather than simply issuing directives.

1   2   3   4   5

5. I believe that leaders in this organization act with integrity, especially when under pressure.

1   2   3   4   5

Foundational Trust Score: _______ / 25

Section 2 — Directional Leadership

6. The organization's purpose and priorities are clear to me and to my colleagues.

1   2   3   4   5

7. I understand how my daily work connects to the organization's larger mission and goals.

1   2   3   4   5

8. When priorities shift, leadership communicates the change clearly and explains the reasoning.

1   2   3   4   5

9. Teams across the organization are working toward aligned goals rather than competing priorities.

1   2   3   4   5

10. Leadership behavior consistently reflects the organization's stated direction — what leaders do matches what they say.

1   2   3   4   5

Directional Leadership Score: _____ / 25

Section 3 — Developmental Culture

11. Collaboration across teams and departments occurs naturally, not just through formal processes or required meetings.

1   2   3   4   5

12. People in this organization feel genuinely valued — for both their contributions and their growth.

1   2   3   4   5

13. New ideas are welcomed and considered seriously, regardless of where in the organization they originate.

1   2   3   4   5

14. When mistakes happen, the response focuses on learning and improvement rather than blame.

1   2   3   4   5

15. The energy and atmosphere of this organization on an ordinary day reflects genuine engagement rather than obligation.

1   2   3   4   5

Developmental Culture Score: _____ / 25

Section 4 — Distributed Capability

16. Leaders in this organization actively develop others — coaching, mentoring, and creating growth opportunities are a regular part of how leadership operates.

    1   2   3   4   5

17. Employees at every level are encouraged to take initiative and make decisions within their areas of responsibility.

    1   2   3   4   5

18. The organization would remain functional and forward-moving if one or two key leaders departed unexpectedly.

    1   2   3   4   5

19. Professional development and growth opportunities exist for people at all levels, not just senior leadership.

    1   2   3   4   5

20. People in this organization think and act like owners — they care about the success of the whole, not just their individual role.

    1   2   3   4   5

Distributed Capability Score: _____ / 25

Scoring Summary

Transfer your scores from each section below.

Foundational Trust   _____ / 25

Directional Leadership   _____ / 25

Developmental Culture   _____ / 25

Distributed Capability _______ / 25

TOTAL _______ / 100

Understanding Your Dimension Scores

Each dimension is scored out of 25. Use the ranges below to interpret your results.

21–25 — This dimension is a current strength.
The architecture in this area is functioning well. Your task is to maintain it — and to notice whether it is compensating for weakness in another dimension.

15–20 — This dimension is developing.
There is real foundation here, but inconsistencies are present. People may experience this area differently depending on their role, their team, or how close they are to senior leadership. Deliberate attention will accelerate progress.

9–14 — This dimension needs attention.
The signals of strain are present and likely visible in the everyday life of the organization, in energy, in alignment, or in momentum. This dimension is placing pressure on the others. Targeted and intentional effort is needed.

5–8 — This dimension requires immediate focus.
The architecture in this area is significantly weakened. The effects are likely showing up in performance, retention, or engagement in ways that are difficult to ignore. This is the place to start.

Understanding Your Overall Score

80–100: Thriving
Your organization's architecture is strong. Trust is well-established, direction is clear, culture is healthy, and leadership capacity is distributed across the system. The signals of organizational health (energy, alignment, and momentum) are likely visible and consistent.

Your priority at this stage is sustainability. Healthy organizations require ongoing attention to remain healthy. The greatest risk at this level is complacency — assuming that because things are working well today, they will continue working well without intentional reinforcement. Keep asking the architectural questions. Keep investing in the dimensions that are performing well, not just the ones that need repair.

The work now is to protect what you have built and deepen it further.

60–79: Progressing

Your organization has real strengths to build on. Some dimensions of the architecture are functioning well, while others are showing signs of strain. You are likely experiencing uneven performance across teams or functions — areas of genuine health sitting alongside areas of visible friction.

The good news is that the foundation exists. The work ahead is one of alignment — identifying where the architecture is tilting and giving those dimensions the focused attention they need. Organizations at this level often have more capacity than they realize. The gap between where you are and where you could be is often shorter than it appears.

The work now is to identify where the architecture needs strengthening and act with intention.

40–59: Unsettled

Something is off, and you likely already know it. The signals of strain (declining energy, fragmenting alignment, stalling momentum) are present and visible. One or more dimensions of the architecture are significantly weakened, and the effects are being felt across the organization even if the root cause has not yet been clearly identified.

This is a critical inflection point. Organizations in this range have not yet reached a crisis, but the trajectory matters enormously. Left unaddressed, the strain tends to compound — weakening dimensions pull the others down, and what begins as architectural imbalance becomes cultural erosion. The right response is not to react to symptoms but to examine the structure honestly and begin the deliberate work of repair.

The work now is to stop managing symptoms and start strengthening the architecture.

20–39: Rebuilding

The architecture of your organization needs significant attention. Trust may be thin, direction unclear, culture strained, or capability concentrated in ways that make the organization fragile. The effects are likely showing up in ways that are hard to ignore — in engagement, in retention, in the quality of everyday interactions, and possibly in performance outcomes.

Rebuilding is not easy work, but it is possible. Organizations have recovered from deeper structural weakness than this. The path forward begins with an honest assessment of where the foundation has eroded and a commitment to rebuilding it — not through a single initiative, but through the consistent, daily leadership behavior that organizational health is ultimately built on.

The work now is to commit to the long work of rebuilding trust, clarity, and capability from the foundation up.

A Note on Using These Results

No single diagnostic captures the full complexity of an organizational system. These results are a starting point — a structured way of surfacing what you may already sense about where your organization is strong and where it is struggling.

The most useful next step is not to react to the overall score but to look carefully at the pattern across dimensions. A low score in Foundational Trust affects everything above it. A low score in Distributed Capability may not be visible in performance today but creates fragility that compounds over time. A strong Culture score alongside a weak Direction score produces warmth without momentum.

The 3D Leadership Architecture is a design tool. These results tell you where the design needs work.

If you would like support in interpreting your results, building a plan to strengthen your organization's architecture, or developing the leadership capacity of your team, 3D Leadership Consulting & Coaching works with organizations at every stage — from those that are thriving and want to sustain it, to those that are rebuilding and need a clear path forward.

The architecture can always be strengthened. The work begins with an honest look at where you are.

Appendix C — The Interdependent Equations

The 3D Leadership Architecture is not a checklist of four independent qualities. It is a structural system — one in which each element depends on and reinforces the others. When all four are functioning, they produce organizational health. When one is missing or weakened, the effects ripple through the entire architecture in predictable ways.

The equations that follow are not mathematical in the strict sense. They are structural. They describe what happens when elements of the architecture are present or absent in combination — and what those combinations produce in the everyday life of an organization.

Read them as a diagnostic lens. If you recognize your organization in one of the deficit equations, you have identified where the architectural work needs to begin.

SECTION 1 — THE FOUNDATION EQUATION

Trust is not one of four equal elements — it is the multiplier that determines the value of everything else.

Foundational Trust × (Directional Leadership + Developmental Culture + Distributed Capability) =Organizational Health

What this means:

> Trust is the multiplier. When it approaches zero, the entire system collapses — regardless of how strong the other dimensions appear.

This is the master equation of the 3D Leadership Architecture. No dimension operates independently. Each one draws its effectiveness from the foundation beneath it and the dimensions around it. The goal is not perfection across all four simultaneously — it is intentional attention to each, knowing that strengthening one strengthens the whole.

SECTION 2 — DIMENSION INTERDEPENDENCY EQUATIONS

What breaks when elements of the architecture are missing — and what it costs the organization.

Directional Leadership − Foundational Trust =Compliance without Commitment

What this means:

People follow the direction — but they don't believe in it.

When leaders set clear direction but haven't established trust, people comply out of obligation rather than conviction. They do what they're told, but they don't invest themselves in it. Engagement is absent. The organization moves, but without real momentum.

Developmental Culture − Directional Leadership =Energy without Purpose

What this means:

A warm, engaged culture that doesn't know where it's going.

Culture without direction produces organizations that feel good but accomplish little. People are connected, collaborative, and motivated — but the energy disperses because there's no shared destination pulling it forward. Warmth without momentum is not organizational health.

Distributed Capability − Developmental Culture =Isolated Expertise

What this means:

Strong individuals who don't develop each other.

When capability is distributed but culture doesn't reinforce collaboration and growth, expertise becomes siloed. People perform within their roles but don't multiply the organization's capacity. Knowledge stays contained rather than shared. Talent concentrates rather than compounds.

Foundational Trust − Directional Leadership =Comfort without Momentum

What this means:

People trust each other — but they're not moving anywhere together.

Trust without direction produces a comfortable but stagnant organization. Relationships are healthy, conflict is low, and people feel safe — but there's no clear destination. The organization drifts rather than advances. Trust is necessary but not sufficient.

Directional Leadership − Distributed Capability =Vision without Execution

What this means:

Clear strategy — that the organization can't carry forward.

Direction without the capability to execute produces frustration at every level. Leaders know where they're going but the organization lacks the distributed leadership capacity to get there. Over-dependence on a few key people creates bottlenecks. Vision stalls at the planning stage.

Developmental Culture − Foundational Trust =Performative Collaboration

What this means:

Teams going through the motions — without genuine psychological safety.

When culture lacks the foundation of trust, collaboration becomes performance. People participate in team rituals but withhold real opinions. Meetings produce consensus without honesty. The appearance of culture exists without its substance. Real development requires real safety.

SECTION 3 — THE SIGNAL EQUATIONS

What the 3D Leadership Architecture produces when dimensions combine — the three signals of organizational health.

Foundational Trust + Directional Leadership =Alignment

What this means:

When people trust leadership and understand the direction, they move together.

Alignment is not agreement. It is coordinated action toward a shared destination. Trust ensures people believe in the direction. Direction ensures people know where to aim their trust. Together they produce an organization where individual effort compounds rather than conflicts.

Foundational Trust + Developmental Culture =Energy

What this means:

> When people feel safe and valued, they bring their full selves to the work.

Organizational energy is not manufactured through initiatives or incentives. It emerges when people feel genuinely trusted and genuinely developed. A culture built on that foundation produces an environment where engagement is the natural state, not the aspiration.

Directional Leadership + Distributed Capability =Momentum

What this means:

> When direction is clear and capability is distributed, the organization moves forward — continuously.

Momentum is sustained organizational movement. It requires knowing where you're going and having the distributed capacity to keep moving even when key people are absent. Direction without capability produces starts and stops. Capability without direction produces motion without progress.

Energy + Alignment + Momentum =Organizational Health

What this means:

> When the full architecture is functioning, the three signals appear — and health is the result.

Organizational health is not a feeling — it is a structural outcome. When all are functioning and aligned, the signals emerge naturally. Energy, Alignment, and Momentum are not goals to pursue. They are evidence that the architecture is working.

SECTION 4 — THE FRAGILITY EQUATION

> High capability without trust creates dependency — not resilience.

Distributed Capability ⁻ Foundational Trust =Fragile Organization

What this means:

> High capability — that was never truly distributed.

This is one of the more dangerous architectural conditions because it looks healthy from the outside. Performance metrics are strong. Capable people are producing results. But without the foundation of trust, capability does not truly distribute — it concentrates in individuals. People perform within their roles rather than developing those around them. Knowledge is hoarded rather than shared. When a key person leaves, the fragility that was hidden beneath the performance suddenly becomes visible — and the organization has no architecture to absorb the loss.

SECTION 5 — THE REBUILDING PRINCIPLE

Strengthening any element of the architecture makes the whole more capable of being strengthened.

What this means:
Each dimension draws its effectiveness from the others.

Organizations under strain often try to fix symptoms in the upper dimensions: launching culture programs, clarifying strategy, building capability initiatives, while the foundation of trust remains compromised. These efforts are unlikely to hold. This is not because there is one correct sequence, but because each dimension draws its effectiveness from the others. Strengthening any single element without attention to the whole is possible and often necessary — but sustainable health requires honest diagnosis of what is actually missing and intentional work across the full architecture.

A Note on Using These Equations

These equations are most useful after you have completed the 3D Leadership Diagnostic (Appendix B) and identified which dimensions of your organization's architecture are under strain. Use the relevant equation not as a verdict, but as a starting point for architectural inquiry: What is actually missing? Where did the deficit begin? What would it take to restore the element that is absent?

The architecture can always be strengthened. The work begins with an honest look at where you are.

Appendix D — Discussion Questions for Academic Use

These questions are designed for seminar discussion, small group conversation, and written reflection in courses covering leadership, organizational behavior, human resource management, organizational development, and related fields. They complement the reflection questions at the close of each chapter, which are written primarily for practicing leaders.

Questions are grouped into three types: Concept Application (engaging directly with the ideas in the chapter), Critical Analysis (examining the framework's assumptions and limitations), and Professional Application (connecting concepts to observed organizational experience).

Introduction — Why Organizational Health Matters

Concept Application

1. The introduction distinguishes between organizational health and organizational performance. In your own words, explain the difference. Why does the author argue that performance metrics alone are insufficient indicators of an organization's condition?

2. The author describes a department characterized by visible disengagement: "motion without momentum, activity without engagement." What structural or leadership conditions might produce this kind of environment? What would need to change for engagement to return?

Critical Analysis

3. The Gallup data cited in the introduction suggests that nearly 80% of employees are disengaged or actively disengaged globally. What are the limitations of self-reported engagement surveys as a measure of organizational health? What might they miss?

Professional Application

4. Think of an organization you have observed — as an employee, volunteer, student worker, or member. Would you describe it as healthy, struggling, or

somewhere in between? What specific behaviors or signals informed your assessment?

Chapter 1 — Performance Is Not Health

Concept Application

1. The author argues that "fear can produce results." Using examples from the chapter, explain how fear-based leadership generates short-term performance while undermining long-term organizational health.

2. The chapter introduces three categories of organizations — thriving, surviving, and struggling. What distinguishes each? Can an organization move between categories? What typically drives that movement?

Critical Analysis

3. The author presents the leader described in Chapter 1 as a complex figure, capable of hearing well-reasoned feedback, yet leading through fear and control. How does this complexity challenge simple narratives about "good" and "bad" leadership? What does it suggest about how organizational dysfunction develops?

Professional Application

4. The chapter describes a "learned calculation" that fear-based cultures produce: Is this worth saying out loud? Describe a situation — real or observed — where you or someone else made this calculation. What were the organizational consequences of staying silent?

Chapter 2 — Understanding Organizational Health

Concept Application

1. The Monday morning meeting scenario presents two organizations facing the same problem with dramatically different outcomes. Identify the specific behaviors in Organization A that distinguish it from Organization B. What structural or cultural conditions make those behaviors possible?

2. Explain the TERA framework (Tribe, Expectation, Rank, Autonomy) in your own words. How does each dimension affect whether people feel safe enough to contribute fully in an organizational setting?

Critical Analysis

3. The author uses a medical analogy to explain organizational health — symptoms are visible, but root causes lie beneath the surface. What are the strengths and limitations of this analogy? In what ways do organizations differ from biological systems?

4. The chapter argues that trust is "a shared confidence in how the system operates" rather than simply a feeling. Do you agree with this definition? What does it imply for how leaders should build and maintain trust?

Professional Application

5. Using the TERA framework, analyze an organization you have been part of. Which of the four dimensions was strongest? Which was weakest? How did that imbalance affect your experience and behavior within the organization?

Chapter 3 — Developmental Culture

Concept Application

1. The author reframes the Drucker quote: "Culture sets the breakfast table and invites Strategy to sit down." What does this reframe add to the original formulation? What does it imply about the relationship between culture and strategic execution?

2. Amy Edmondson's research on psychological safety is referenced in this chapter. Define psychological safety in your own words and explain how it connects to the concept of developmental culture as described by the author.

Critical Analysis

3. The chapter argues that culture is the "enabling dimension" of the 3D Leadership Architecture. Do you agree that culture carries more weight than the other dimensions? What evidence supports or challenges this claim?

4. The Costco and Mayo Clinic examples are used to illustrate culture at scale. What are the risks of using large, well-known organizations as models for culture? What might smaller or less resourced organizations learn — or not learn — from these examples?

Professional Application

5. The chapter describes intentional culture-building practices: the Innovation Summit, post-event debriefs, recognition in staff meetings. Design one culture-reinforcing practice for a hypothetical organization you are leading. What signal would it send, and how would you sustain it over time?

Chapter 4 — Directional Leadership

Concept Application

1. The chapter distinguishes between compliance and commitment. Define each in your own words and explain why the author argues that direction — rather than incentives or authority — is what produces genuine commitment.

2. Kennedy's moon speech and Nadella's reorientation of Microsoft are both presented as examples of directional leadership. What do these two cases have in common? What is different about the contexts in which direction was provided?

Critical Analysis

3. The chapter argues that "direction does not suppress engagement — it channels it." Under what conditions might this claim be challenged? Can strong direction suppress engagement? What factors determine the difference?

4. The author presents four disciplines of directional leadership: clarity before communication, consistency over time, purpose alongside destination, and invitation over imposition. Which might be most difficult to practice consistently, and why?

Professional Application

5. The chapter asks: if you asked ten people on your team to describe where the organization is heading, how similar would their answers be? Estimate

what you would find in an organization you know. What does your estimate reveal about the directional clarity of that organization's leadership?

Chapter 5 — Distributed Capability

Concept Application

1. The All Blacks example introduces the idea that leadership is a system rather than a position. What does it mean for an organization to treat leadership as a system? What structures, practices, and cultural norms make that possible?

2. The chapter introduces "broadening experiences" as a vehicle for leadership development. How does this approach differ from traditional leadership training programs? What are its advantages and limitations?

Critical Analysis

3. A coaching culture is presented as a structural advantage rather than a soft organizational nicety. What distinguishes a genuine coaching culture from an organization that uses coaching language without changing its underlying dynamics?

4. The chapter argues that distributed capability is harder to build but "nearly impossible to break." Do you agree? What evidence from the chapter — or from your own observation — supports or challenges this claim?

Professional Application

5. The chapter identifies two forms of fragility created by concentrated leadership: departure risk and decision bottleneck. Describe an organization you have observed that experienced one of these. What were the symptoms? What would distributed capability have changed?

Chapter 6 — When the Architecture Breaks Down

Concept Application

1. The chapter presents three imbalance patterns: direction without culture, culture without direction, and leadership without capability. For each

pattern, identify the specific organizational symptoms the author describes and explain the underlying mechanism that produces them.

2. The chapter argues that organizational problems are "rarely individual performance" and almost always "architectural imbalance." What does this diagnostic shift — from people to structure — require of leaders? Why does the author suggest it is one of the harder moves a leader can make?

Critical Analysis

3. The author introduces "pressure is a privilege" as a reframe for organizational resilience. Under what conditions is this reframe useful? Under what conditions might it be harmful or dismissive of genuine organizational strain?

4. The chapter opens with a scenario in which a supervisor blames an employee for a reasonable judgment call made under real constraints. What organizational conditions make this kind of misdiagnosis common? What would need to change for the diagnosis to start with structure rather than people?

Professional Application

5. Using the three imbalance patterns described in this chapter, diagnose an organization you have observed. Which pattern best describes its current condition? What evidence supports your diagnosis? What would you recommend as a first step toward rebalancing the architecture?

Chapter 7 — Signals of Organizational Health

Concept Application

1. The chapter identifies three signals of organizational health: energy, alignment, and momentum. Define each in behavioral terms — what would you actually observe in a healthy organization that demonstrates each signal is present?

2. The chapter argues that alignment is frequently misunderstood — that it does not mean agreement. Explain the distinction the author draws. Why does this distinction matter for how leaders manage disagreement and dissent?

Critical Analysis

3. The author claims that organizational health "reveals itself through the energy of everyday work" rather than through reports and dashboards. What are the advantages of using observational signals as diagnostics? What are the risks?

4. The chapter suggests that each fading signal points toward a specific weakening dimension. How useful is this diagnostic mapping? What are its limitations?

Professional Application

5. The chapter describes the experience of walking into two very different organizational environments and sensing the difference immediately. Describe an organization you have entered where the atmosphere told you something immediately about its health. What specific signals did you notice? What did they suggest about the underlying architecture?

Chapter 8 — Designing Healthy Organizations

Concept Application

1. The chapter argues that organizational health begins with "how leaders show up," through small, daily, consistent behaviors rather than grand initiatives. How does this claim connect to the broader argument of the book? What does it imply about the relationship between leadership behavior and organizational culture?

2. The chapter presents four parallel statements: a conversation handled with respect strengthens trust; a leader who listens openly strengthens culture; a decision explained clearly strengthens direction; a mentor who invests in someone's growth strengthens capability. For each statement, identify a specific leadership behavior it implies and explain the mechanism by which that behavior produces the stated outcome.

Critical Analysis

3. The book as a whole argues that organizational health is a matter of intentional design. What does this claim assume about the degree of control

leaders have over organizational systems? What factors might limit a leader's ability to design the organization they intend?

4. The chapter argues that culture, once genuinely established, generates its own momentum and sustains itself without constant leadership investment. Is this claim realistic? Under what conditions might a healthy culture sustain itself, and under what conditions might it require ongoing active maintenance?

Professional Application

5. The book closes with the argument that "every leader, at every level, has the opportunity to help build" a healthy organization. Do you agree that distributed leadership responsibility extends to every level? What are the implications of this argument for how we think about accountability, authority, and organizational change?

Appendix C — The Interdependent Equations

Concept Application

1. The appendix presents six deficit equations — combinations of dimensions where one element is absent. Choose two deficit equations and describe what each condition would look like in a real organization. What specific behaviors or dynamics would signal that an organization is experiencing that particular imbalance?

Critical Analysis

2. The Fragility Equation argues that distributed capability without foundational trust produces an organization that looks healthy from the outside but isn't. Evaluate this claim. What evidence from the book supports it? Do you find it convincing, and under what conditions might it be challenged?

Professional Application

3. Using the Signal Equations, assess an organization you have been part of. Which signal — Alignment, Energy, or Momentum — was strongest? Which was weakest or absent? What does the corresponding equation suggest about which architectural element needed the most attention?

These discussion questions may be reproduced for educational use with appropriate attribution to the source text.

Acknowledgments

No leadership journey is built alone, and this book reflects the influence of many people who have shaped how I think about leadership, culture, and organizational health.

First, I want to express my deepest appreciation to my family: my wife Kristen, my daughter Holly, and my son Evan and his wife Kymberly. Their encouragement, patience, and support made this work possible and continue to remind me that the most important leadership lessons often begin at home.

I am also grateful for the many leaders, mentors, and friends who have generously shared their insights and encouragement over the years. Leadership is always a learning journey, and I am especially thankful to my Vice President for nine years, Kelly Kerner, who instinctively and consistently modeled the very leadership behaviors described in this book.

Finally, I want to thank the colleagues and teams I have had the privilege of working alongside throughout my career. Their commitment to the people they served, to one another, and to meaningful work continually reinforced my belief that healthy organizations are built through trust, collaboration, and shared leadership.

Any insights contained in these pages are shaped by their influence, though any shortcomings remain my own.

About the Author

Scott Williams is a leadership advisor, executive coach, and the founder of 3D Leadership Consulting & Coaching. He is the creator of the 3D Leadership Architecture, a framework that helps leaders and organizations intentionally design healthy systems through directional leadership, developmental culture, and distributed capability.

Scott's work is grounded in more than three decades of executive leadership experience across several major research universities, including twenty-five years as Executive Director of the University of Georgia Career Center, where his team earned multiple national awards for innovation, technology, and excellence, and sustained a 95% average Career Outcomes Rate over the last decade. He is the 2025 recipient of the SoACE Southern Star Award, recognizing sustained and outstanding contributions to the profession.

Through consulting, speaking, and coaching, he works with leaders and organizations seeking to create environments where people can contribute fully and where meaningful work can flourish.

Learn more about Scott's work at 3DLeadershipCoaching.com

Notes

— 116 —

Notes